re
probl
solving

Prentice Hall
BUSINESS

Books that make you better

Books that make you better. That make you *be* better, *do* better, *feel* better. Whether you want to upgrade your personal skills or change your job, whether you want to improve your managerial style, become a more powerful communicator, or be stimulated and inspired as you work.

Prentice Hall Business is leading the field with a new breed of skills, careers and development books. Books that are a cut above the mainstream – in topic, content and delivery – with an edge and verve that will make you better, with less effort.

Books that are as sharp and smart as you are.

Prentice Hall Business.
We work harder – so you don't have to.

For more details on products, and to contact us, visit
www.business-minds.com
www.yourmomentum.com

Pearson
Education

■ *real* skills for *real* results ■

real
problem
solving

how to unblock thinking
and make obstacles
disappear

JK SMART

Prentice
Hall

BUSINESS

PEARSON EDUCATION LIMITED

Head Office:
Edinburgh Gate
Harlow CM20 2JE
Tel: +44 (0)1279 623623
Fax: +44 (0)1279 431059

London Office:
128 Long Acre
London WC2E 9AN
Tel: +44 (0)20 7447 2000
Fax: +44 (0)20 7447 2170
Websites: www.business-minds.com
          www.yourmomentum.com

First published in Great Britain in 2003

© Pearson Education Limited 2003

The right of JK Smart to be identified as author of this work has been asserted
by her in accordance with the Copyright, Designs and Patents Act 1988.

ISBN 0 273 66330 5

British Library Cataloguing in Publication Data
A CIP catalogue record for this book can be obtained from the British Library

10 9 8 7 6 5 4 3 2 1

Designed by Claire Brodmann Book Designs, Lichfield, Staffs
Typeset by Northern Phototypesetting Co. Ltd, Bolton
Printed and bound in Great Britain by Bell & Bain Ltd, Glasgow

The publishers' policy is to use paper manufactured from sustainable forests.

To Rachael, for making my biggest problem
disappear and for enabling me to take
the road less travelled.

With thanks to Stuart, not only for all his help
with the book but for his openness, honesty,
mathematician's perspective, passion for Wolves,
Black-Country pessimism and wry humour, which
provided the perfect 'soundtrack' to the writing.

Contents

CONTENTS

About the author

Karen Smart's background is in individual and organizational development. However, unlike some in her field, first and foremost Karen sees herself as a line manager. In recent years, she's worked primarily on enabling managers to manage – developing and delivering everything from individual skill building and management development programmes to management systems design and organization wide culture change. In addition to managing her team, Karen has coached senior managers and facilitated cross-functional working, problem solving and conflict management. Although she has two degrees and has researched extensively across a range of disciplines, ultimately Karen feels she's learned most about management from her experience as an overworked and undervalued manager, disempowered by bureaucracy. From this experience – and inspired by the man she says 'puts the J into JK Smart and a lot of the smart too' – the philosophy of *real* management for *real* people was born.

■ *real* management for the way it is ■

Introduction to *real* management

▶ Welcome to the *real* world

Do you read most management books and say, 'If only it was that easy in the real world'? *Real* management is the answer for every manager who knows it's about doing the best we can with what we've got, in the real world of organizations that are demanding more and more for less and less. It's for real managers who think the books we've read must have been written by people who don't live in our world and who mistake us for superheroes. We know we could work out a better way of managing if only we could get off the treadmill long enough to find the time.

▶ Telling it like it is

But what if someone had read everything, tried everything, worked out why things don't work in the real world, found a way of managing that works with the complexity of real life instead of pretending it's simple, and then taken time off from managing to tell you about it? And what if that someone wasn't a guru, academic or consultant but an ordinary, overworked manager who knows what managers are up against and who doesn't judge or preach or try to get people to be something they're not? And what if that same manager understood that the idea of 'one size fits all' doesn't work and offered you a way of blending her insight with your experience so you could become the manager you were meant to be?

Real management:

- Makes sense of your experience by explaining why, when we do things by the book, they don't work.

- Is based on a common-sense understanding of human nature that takes your concerns seriously and starts from the assumption that what you're doing now makes sense for the situation you're in.

- Helps you turn your past experience into the key that unlocks your best ever management performance.

1

Confessions of an overworked manager

Towards a new way of managing in the *real* world

I'm tired of being overworked – are you?

I'm not a management guru. I'm an overworked manager who got sick of being overworked. I love my work so I give it 100 per cent . . . I push my team . . . we achieve things . . . I'm given more work . . . I give it 110 per cent . . . I push my team a bit harder . . . we achieve more things . . . I'm given more work . . . need I go on? Stress researchers say our automatic response to overload is to do what we were doing before only harder and for longer. Psychologists say insanity is doing the same things over and over and expecting different results. So, as they say in America, 'You do the math!'

There has to be a better way of working

Psychologists also say that if you want a different result, you have to do something different. Since I started my management career, I've seen (and been guilty of) the sorry way managers treat their staff (and vice versa), and I've become increasingly disillusioned with the established wisdom about managing people. I began to believe there had to be a better way.

> **Beliefs** are thoughts we use to guide our decisions and actions, although we tend to forget and see them as indisputable facts. With any action, a belief always comes first. We find evidence to support our beliefs in our experience. Once we've got a belief, we tend not to question it, unless an experience forces us to.

People shouldn't have to leave their brains at the door or become robots when they come into work. They shouldn't have to run ever harder just to stand still. In recent years, I've watched people go sick with stress and I've seen stress-management programmes being offered as the cure, all the time thinking that we must be in big trouble if we're settling for *managing* stress instead of removing it at source. I knew there had to be a way to remove the stress caused by the gap between who we are outside of work and who we have to be at work. There had to be a way of managing that isn't soul-destroying for everyone involved. I just didn't know what that way was. Then I met someone who changed the way I think about people; who motivated me to find a new way of managing; who influenced me to want to be a better manager; and who inspired me to take time out and write this series of books in the hope that I could do for others what he did for me.

There had to be a way of managing that isn't soul-destroying for everyone involved.

Getting out of the box of traditional management thinking

I started as a management trainee on a year's development programme, during which I became fascinated by the way people manage, and I've been a student of management as well as a manager ever since. I'm exaggerating (but, sadly, only slightly) when I say that by the time I decided there had to be a better way, I'd already read and tried everything ever published about management. Clearly, if I wanted new answers I had to look in new places. Not one to do things by halves, I've looked close to management, in neuroscience, psychology and psychotherapy to learn how our brains work, why we do the things we do, and how to deal with emotions and the effects of early conditioning on our behaviour. And I've looked far from management – everything from aikido to Zen Buddhism via horticulture and homoeopathy (well, if we aren't growing something as managers, we're curing it, right?). And yes, I confess, I've read almost everything the self-help movement has to offer, sifting the sensible from the senseless.

Looking for what makes sense

After years of being a task-focused manager working for organizations in 'initiative' mode, I can assure you I'm too sceptical about the 'next new idea' and the 'one size fits all' solution to have bought into any one set of beliefs. Instead, what I've done is collect and use the ideas that made sense of my experience. Small sentence, big idea, so let me say it again. I researched a wide range of subjects and whenever I got a feeling of 'that's obvious', I applied the idea to the way I manage and used my experience to figure out what worked.

> **Trial and error** is how we learn from experience – trying to do something, noticing what doesn't work, and changing our approach until we find what works. More often than not, we decide what works and doesn't work based on the feedback we get.

I want to make it easier for you than it was for me

It would be hypocritical for me to tell you I'm sceptical of people who sell you the 'one right way' and then try to do the same thing myself, so that's not what I'm doing. I'm sharing what I've learned to save you having to do all the research I did. But I can't do it all for you – we have to be in it together.

Equal partners or no deal

Ninety-five per cent of what we learn comes from experience, with only five per cent coming from books, training, etc., and they only work when they resonate with our own experience by triggering memories of earlier experiences.

> We have vast quantities of experience that we can't hold in our **conscious minds** so we store these experiences in our subconscious. The trouble with our **subconscious** is that it's sub (below) conscious (the level of our awareness) so we aren't conscious of (don't know) what's in there. We need triggers to surface it.

A good book is, in effect, telling you something you already know intuitively; you just haven't articulated it on a conscious level.

Intuition is that feeling of knowing something, without knowing how you know it. It means you're using information from your subconscious mind that your conscious mind isn't aware of.

What I'm telling you will work only if you use my insight as a trigger for surfacing your experience and intuitive (subconscious) insight because, in the end, only your insight can improve your performance. It's 'equal partnership learning' – I provide the trigger, you provide the experience. I have no ambition to create clones of me. I want people to manage in a way that works for them – a way that suits their unique blend of insight and experience. What I *am* hoping for, though, is that you'll think what I'm saying is common sense.

Common sense (a rarity in life) is when something is both logical (appealing to our conscious minds) and intuitive (appealing to our subconscious minds) and we get a 'that's obvious' feeling. When our conscious and subconscious minds are out of sync, we get an 'off' feeling – something isn't quite right, but we don't know why.

So, as you read this book, think about your experience and see if you get a 'that's obvious' feeling. If you do, then try my approach, learn from it, and adapt it to meet your needs. If you get an 'off' feeling, then challenge what I'm saying, come to your own insight, try that, learn from it, and adapt it to meet your needs.

Starting from where people are

The biggest mistake people make when trying to help move someone forward is to assume they're both starting from the same place – something that never happens in real life. I don't want to make that mistake with you, so throughout this book – in shaded boxes – I explain the concepts and beliefs that underpin my approach to management. In the Appendix, there's also a broader look at where I'm coming from as a manager.

Let's keep it real here

If you're like most managers I know, you won't have time to read a heavyweight volume (even if I had time to write one), but you won't want to be fobbed off with one-minute answers that only work in books either. So what I've done (to give you the best of both worlds) is to put some powerful messages – that hopefully will resonate with your own experience and trigger your insight – into a quick but intense read. There's also a reminder of the key messages and some questions to think about at the end of each chapter.

Let me know what you think

I mean what I say about being equal partners, so if you want to share your experience and insight or ask questions about any-thing in the book, I'd really like to hear from you. You can email me at **JKSmartBooks@aol.com**. I take on a few telephone coaching clients each year so managers who are interested may email me as may trainers and development specialists who are interested in attending an 'equal partners learning programme' to be licensed to work with this material.

IN SHORT

▶ We can't keep doing what we've always been doing because it doesn't work and it stresses us out in the process.

▶ People who still tout the established management wisdom are 'flat earthers' who need to be challenged to develop an approach that works in the real world.

▶ I'm not telling you anything you don't already know: I'm only helping you to bring your insight to the surface where you can do something with it.

▶ Challenge everything I say, and take away only what makes sense of your experience.

2

The key to unlocking your best ever performance

Track back from your experience, then work forward from your beliefs

We already have everything we need to be effective

We just have preferences for, and are more skilled in, some things than others (a result of them being our preferences). Development, especially in people skills, isn't about teaching new skills as much as about unblocking existing ones. What blocks our development? Our beliefs, which govern how we use our characteristics. Lack of self-belief is the single biggest block to excellent performance. Once you get that sorted, everything else falls into place.

But our beliefs hinder us from using them

You may have excellent communication skills, but if you believe that talking never solved anything, then they're not likely to get much of an outing, so how will you ever know just how good they are? Have you ever thought, 'I wish I could do that but I'm not confident/bright/calm/etc. enough'? What are the component parts of the skill you wish you had? Do you use them in any other activity or part of your life?

And so do our judgements about ourselves

What's your biggest strength? Okay, in what kinds of situations does it really help you to perform well? Now identify at least one situation in which it hinders your performance. You may find this hard, but persevere, because I guarantee there will be at least one. If in doubt, ask a trusted colleague. Now, relabel the strength as a neutral word or phrase that would apply equally to both the helpful and hindering situations. When you've done that, try the same exercise again but this time for your biggest weakness and, suddenly, we don't have strengths and weaknesses any more; we have characteristics.

> A **characteristic** is a piece of knowledge, an attitude, a behaviour, a skill, or any single input you bring to your performance. It is described neutrally to avoid implying strength or weakness. For example, I'm not lazy, I'm someone who doesn't like to waste energy. The same characteristic can be helpful or hindering depending on the context in which it is used.

The need to find and challenge our hindering beliefs

Are you happy with your results in all areas of your life? People are happy with their performance when the external world matches their inner reality and unhappy when it doesn't.

My definition of **sanity** is when the external world matches the picture of it that we have in our minds without us having to distort either what's out there or what's in our minds. It's when we see things as they are, not as we wish they were.

There are people who are happy or unhappy for healthy reasons (they see things as they really are and not as they'd like them to be). There are also people who are happy (but delusional) or unhappy (but victims) for unhealthy reasons (they distort what they see to conform to their inner reality).

Our **subconscious creates experiences** for us (from events) that reinforce what we believe about the world and the people in it, if necessary by distorting the picture so we see only what we want to see. But, while it does this to keep us feeling sane on a day-to-day basis (yes, even when all around us think we're delusional), it craftily creates negative experiences when it wants to push us into re-examining our beliefs. And if we don't re-examine our beliefs after a negative experience, it keeps recreating the same experience until we give in and do what it wants.

Effectiveness is when people are happy for healthy reasons. If you're not happy with the responses you're getting and the experiences you're creating, then you have three choices:

1. Carry on as you are, a victim in your own melodrama, blaming circumstances or other people and dragging the rest of us down with you.

2. Reframe the results so that you turn them into a positive experience that you can be happy about.

> **Reframing** is when we change our interpretation of an event, usually by challenging the beliefs that underpin our original interpretation. We do this by finding other ways of looking at it.

3. Assume what you got was what you wanted and track back to the beliefs that drove the behaviour. If you're okay with the beliefs, then go back to option 2. If you're not, then re-examine them and develop alternatives to change your behaviour and achieve different results.

We all know how to do option 1 but what about the rest? Easier said than done? Yes, if you associate change with behaviour change, but I'm talking about belief changes that take milliseconds to achieve and last forever and – and this is the big plus – a changed belief triggers a changed behaviour in ways that don't require mountains of will-power to sustain. Want to give it a try? Read on . . .

A changed belief triggers a changed behaviour without requiring mountains of willpower.

IN SHORT

- You've got everything you need already; it's only your beliefs that are holding you back.
- Stop being so hard on yourself: being judgemental and self-critical never helped anyone improve.
- Take the acid test: ask yourself if you're happy with the results that you are achieving.

▶ If you're not happy, don't just sit there; do something
about it.

3

If it's as easy as the books make out, why are there so many books?

Resisting the temptation to want easy answers in a complex world

It's not my fault – it's the way I'm programmed

It's scientific fact, mother! Wanting easy answers doesn't make me lazy. Brains are hard-wired to lay down programmes in our subconscious so we can do things without thinking (on autopilot, if you like), leaving us with plenty of spare capacity to deal with the unexpected.

The brain develops **programmes** in our subconscious, based on our experiences. When it registers an unfamiliar event, it quickly (so quickly we don't know it's happening) looks for a suitable pre-existing programme (**pre-programme** for short) to interpret the event (like a computer matching fingerprints). When it registers a good enough match, it automatically triggers the response from the earlier experience.

Trainers call the pre-programmes that serve us well 'unconscious competence'.

> At the bottom of the learning ladder is **unconscious incompetence** (when we don't know what we don't know), then **conscious incompetence** (when we realize we need to learn something), followed by **conscious competence** (when we're mastering a skill and still have to concentrate all the time we're doing it). This stage continues until we can do it without having to think (**unconscious competence**). Driving is the classic example.

So many choices – so little time

The trouble with being an overworked manager is that the only time I get a taste of the huge variety today's world has to offer is when I'm skimming the Sunday papers, and let's face it, who has time to do more than skim when there's so many sections? I used to like that line in Kipling's *If* about filling the unforgiving minute with 60 seconds' worth of distance run . . . until I had to live it! Ignoring the fact that some of today's time-saving devices don't actually do what they say on the tin (I'd mention email, but don't get me started on that or we'll be here all day), it's the ever increasing expectations of what we're meant to do with the time we save that get me. It's as though if we're not working flat out to improve the quality of our relationships, bodies, spirits and lifestyles – and don't forget careers – then we're somehow failing to make the most of everything that twenty-first-century life has to offer.

Is it any surprise that, as managers, we want one-minute answers to twenty-year problems? Who has time to spend with their staff these days, when the pressure to deliver more outputs with fewer resources is greater than ever? No wonder hypocrisy creeps in, as on a recent appraisal training course, where a group of management-level appraisees had no problem saying that for their own appraisal they wanted their manager to take as much time as it needed to do a good job, but that they were far too busy to do that for their team members.

The customer is king – so give them what they want

An IT manager asked me to approve a plan for recruiting IT officers for a number of local offices around the country. He wanted to run the selection process at HQ, with IT experts interviewing and then allocating successful candidates to local managers. He wanted the recruits to have high-quality IT skills, and he knew local managers weren't IT literate enough to ensure that. Something wasn't right with his proposal (my 'off' feeling), so I probed and discovered he feared local managers wouldn't have ownership of the national IT strategy if they'd had no say in the appointment of their IT officer. In the end, we recruited at local level with an IT person doing the shortlist (for quality control) and asking the technical questions, but with the local line manager making the final decision. The solution gave the IT manager everything he needed, which he wouldn't have got if I'd just given him what he wanted.

A lot of organizations buy into the 'customer is king' myth, and so must many management writers, otherwise quick-fix, autopilot, 'one-size-fits-all' solutions wouldn't be so prevalent on the management shelves of your local bookstore. Books that offer solutions that would insult your intelligence if you weren't so distracted by the demands of your job. Solutions that *do* insult your subconscious intelligence if only you had time to listen to it. And when you *do* look beyond the glib answers, what do you find? A complex world overcomplicated by impenetrable academics or the fashionable world of the latest management guru who thinks you can solve everything by applying an alarmingly alliterative acronym!

We need *real* answers for the way it is in the *real* world

Real managers run a mile from formulaic approaches that treat human beings as a constant when they're a variable. We know people make money by giving us what we want regardless of whether it's what we need, but in the *real* world what's important is what works, not what's quick. We need to find a way to meet our conscious need for easy answers with our subconscious need for a common-sense approach that works with the complexity of human nature.

IN SHORT

- We may be programmed to want easy answers, but we don't have to give in to temptation.
- We have so many choices about how to spend our time that it makes sense not to waste time getting our people management wrong.
- What we want isn't always what we need, so we need to think before we buy what's on offer.

▶ Yes, we *want* easy answers, but we *need* answers that work, so let's not settle for shabby compromise: let's get the best of both worlds.

the way it is ■ *real* management for the way it is ■ *real* management for the way it is ■ r
■ *real* management for the way it is ■ *real* management for the way it is ■ *real* managem
nagement for the way it is ■ *real* management for the way it is ■ *real* management for the
the way it is ■ *real* management for the way it is ■ *real* management for the way it is ■ re
■ *real* management for the way it is ■ *real* management for the way it is ■ *real* managem
agement for the way it is ■ *real* management for the way it is ■ *real* management for the
the way it is ■ *real* management

PART

1

management for the way it is ■ re
■ *real* management for the way it is ■ *real* for the way it is ■ *real* managem
management for the way it is ■ *real* mana it is ■ *real* management for the
the way it is ■ *real* management for the nagement for the way it is ■ re
■ *real* management for the way it is ■ for the way it is ■ *real* managem
agement for the way it is ■ *real* manage it is ■ *real* management for the
the way it is ■ *real* management for the way anagement for the way it is ■ re
■ *real* management for the way it is ■ *real* for the way it is ■ *real* managem
agement for the way it is ■ *real* management it is ■ *real* management for the
the way it is ■ *real* management for the way it management for the way it is ■ re
■ *real* management for the way it is ■ *real* man for the way it is ■ *real* managem
agement for the way it is ■ *real* management it is ■ *real* management for the
the way it is ■ *real* management for the way it is anagement for the way it is ■ re
■ *real* management for the way it is ■ *real* man for the way it is ■ *real* managem
agement for the way it is ■ *real* management it is ■ *real* management for the
the way it is ■ *real* management for the way it is ■ management for the way it is ■ re
■ *real* management for the way it is ■ *real* management for the way it is ■ *real* managem
agement for the way it is ■ *real* management for the way it is ■ *real* management for the
the way it is ■ *real* management for the way it is ■ *real* management for the way it is ■ r
■ *real* management for the way it is ■ *real* management for the way it is ■ *real* managem
agement for the way it is ■ *real* management for the way it is ■ *real* management for the
the way it is ■ *real* management for the way it is ■ *real* management for the way it is ■ r
■ *real* management for the way it is ■ *real* management for the way it is ■ *real* managem
anagement for the way it is ■ *real* management for the way it is ■ *real* management for th
the way it is ■ *real* management for the way it is ■ *real* management for the way it is ■ re
■ *real* management for the way it is ■ *real* management for the way it is ■ *real* managem
agement for the way it is ■ *real* management for the way it is ■ *real* management for th
the way it is ■ *real* management for the way it is ■ *real* management for the way it is ■ re
■ *real* management for the way it is ■ *real* management for the way it is ■ *real* managem
anagement for the way it is ■ *real* management for the way it is ■ *real* management for th
the way it is ■ ■ *real* **management for the way it is** ■ *real* management for the way it is ■ r
■ *real* management for the way it is ■ *real* management for the way it is ■ *real* managem
anagement for the way it is ■ *real* management for the way it is ■ *real* management for th
the way it is ■ *real* management for the way it is ■ *real* management for the way it is ■ re
■ *real* management for the way it is ■ *real* management for the way it is ■ *real* managem
anagement for the way it is ■ *real* management for the way it is ■ *real* management for th
the way it is ■ *real* management for the way it is ■ *real* management for the way it is ■ re
■ *real* management for the way it is ■ *real* management for the way it is ■ *real* manage
anagement for the way it is ■ *real* management for the way it is ■ *real* management for th
the way it is ■ *real* management for the way it is ■ *real* management for the way it is ■ r
■ *real* management for the way it is ■ *real* management for the way it is ■ *real* manage
anagement for the way it is ■ *real* management for the way it is ■ *real* management for th
the way it is ■ *real* management for the way it is ■ *real* management for the way it is ■ r
■ *real* management for the way it is ■ *real* management for the way it is ■ *real* managem
anagement for the way it is ■ *real* management for the way it is ■ *real* management for th
the way it is ■ *real* management for the way it is ■ *real* management for the way it is ■

Understanding why problem solving goes wrong so you can put it right

▶ **Understanding the cause-and-effect relationships**

As an overworked manager, I find it easy to get sucked into dealing with problems at symptom level rather than root cause. I get a buzz out of taking decisive action so I find it hard to slow down and make the effort to understand why something has gone wrong, even though I know the buzz won't last any longer than my solution.

▶ **Taking a long hard look at the way we solve problems**

If you're anything like me, you'll be itching to get straight to the 'how to do it' part. But remember, that's where we went wrong in the past, so please bear with me because we can't put something right unless we understand why it went wrong in the first place. In a quick read, I don't have time to give you lots of examples plus my insights, so I'm going to explore one big example in depth. I've used a composite of several real-life experiences, so I can highlight the issues that undermine our approach to problem solving.

4

Why do problems never seem to go away?

Drinking from the poisoned chalice and living to tell the tale

Say hello to Steve and his big problem

Steve was the harassed manager in charge of the customer-liaison team who were responsible for ensuring multi-disciplinary projects in our organization were delivered on time, within budget, to specification with satisfied customers. I say that, but it would be more accurate to say he was in charge of the people who got the blame when things went wrong. Steve wasn't alone in that though. Most managers spend our working lives dealing with the problems caused when things don't go the way they're supposed to – whether they're problems with the work itself or with the people we have to deal with to get the job done.

Steve's problem was especially enticing because it wrapped up all the things we think of as problems in their own right into one big, juicy problem. Like:

■ When things don't go the way we want them to – it was bad enough for Steve that the projects his team managed failed but then he had all the people problems that were part of the fallout.

- When every trick in the book has been tried and failed and we haven't got a creative solution left in us – this problem had been going on for years, so Steve was worried there wasn't anything new left to try.

- When we have a number of different ways forward and can't decide which to take – Steve couldn't decide whether to try to solve the problem himself or set up yet another problem-solving group.

- When we know where we need to get to but our path is littered with obstacles – Steve knew what success would look like and previous failures had given him a clear idea of what the obstacles were.

This is just an everyday story of the problems you get when there's a lack of co-operation between departments who are meant to be pulling together. It may well be a familiar scenario – if you don't work in an organization with departments then chances are you still work with other people and teams to achieve your goals. So you are still likely to have the kind of problems that Steve had.

There's always more to a problem than what's on the surface

Steve's problem reminded me of the time I bought a house with an eighty-foot garden, half of which was (inexplicably) concreted over. I decided it had to go so I hired a skip and a pneumatic drill and invited my brother to help. If I'd known we'd eventually fill nine skips before we hit soil, I'd have covered it with gravel and bought a few planters instead!

About eighteen months ago in a blaze of internal publicity, the various department heads had come up with a package of measures to solve this particular problem. They hadn't worked . . . and Steve thought he knew why.

- They'd worked on the problem without defining it properly and jumped to a solution without any analysis – with disastrous results.
- They'd failed to involve the people affected by the problem so no one else had any ownership of it.
- They'd tried to tackle a problem that went beyond their remit.
- They all had their pet solutions that they stuck to like glue but never managed to find convincing arguments for them.
- They had differing perceptions on what the problem was that weren't understood by the other parties.
- No one managed to break down the inter-departmental barriers.
- Fears (of making mistakes and getting blamed) weren't faced but still influenced their choice of solutions.
- Their lack of problem-solving skills meant they got to solutions in dubious ways.
- Their implementation planning consisted of dumping a set of outline proposals onto their direct reports.
- There'd been no improvement in performance since then. If anything, things had got worse as middle managers and front-line staff became demoralized by the changes.

But this wasn't why Steve had come to me for help. He was worried about the effect our culture would have on his ability to solve problems. According to Steve, you couldn't find a more risk-averse, keep-your-head-below-the parapet, blame-culture than ours. Or a more controlling corporate centre, who made the customer-facing departments more account- able to them than their customers. Or a hierarchy more dom- inated by people who'd been promoted for their professional not managerial skills. He'd been with the organization for years and, from the way he talked, I thought my team must be the only one in the whole place who *didn't* get into trouble for the risks we took and the mistakes we made. Anyway, this is about Steve's perceptions so let me just say that I can remem- ber, as clearly as if it was yesterday, thinking 'this is solvable' . . . but I'm blowed if I can remember why.

A little knowledge is a dangerous thing

Like all managers, I've spent most of my career solving prob- lems. I've come into new jobs to find poorly performing teams and a shedload of things going wrong so I've had my fair share of experience of both task and people

I've yet to come across a problem that wasn't a people problem.

problems. I've yet to come across a problem that wasn't a people problem because even the most one-dimen- sional task-based problem usually turned out to be a case of people not getting their thinking straight. And in my search for the holy grail of management effectiveness I'd read every book ever written (I'm exaggerat- ing but not as much as I wish I was) and asked everyone I'd met for their methods. I'd never found one that worked but I knew a lot about what doesn't.

But Oscar Wilde isn't the only one who can resist anything but temptation

As problems go, this was complex, long-standing, inter- departmental, high-risk, affecting many people in different ways and connected to a range of other problems. Still, as I told Steve, no matter how daft it looks, people had to be doing what made sense to them so the way to solve their problem was to find their logic.

> I use the term **logic** to mean our unique concept of rational cause and effect. Everyone has their own logic, so if you work backwards from the effects people achieve and ask yourself why someone would want to do that you will find the belief that caused them to produce that effect – that's their logic.

Some talented people had sustained this problem for years, which confirmed my belief that people don't fail; we just materialize intentions we didn't know we had. If we understood what they gained from not solving the problem, finding the solution would be child's play. We'd be heroes. How could we resist? How could anyone resist?

IN SHORT

- **Look before you leap.** How many times have you taken on a problem without thinking through whether you are the right person for the job?
- **Inter-departmental problems need particularly careful handling.** What's your experience of inter-departmental conflict?
- **Understand why previous solutions didn't work.** Have you ever tried to solve a long-standing problem without taking a long hard look at its history?
- **People do what makes sense.** Have you ever wondered how people manage to get themselves into the situations you find them in?

5

Why is it always the other guy's fault?

Gathering all the perspectives and hoping the truth is out there

Different department or different planet?

I needed to understood the different 'logics' of the different stakeholders so I could help Steve produce a solution that would please everyone.

> I divide **stakeholders** into **interest and impact groups**. Impact groups can prevent you achieving the outcomes. Interest groups will be affected by the outcome but can't prevent you achieving the outcomes. You can't ignore the needs of either group, but the distinction helps when you're managing a conflict of interests.

The easiest way to understand someone's logic is to ask them, so I did – in a roundabout way. What an eye-opener. You know when two people come out of a meeting and tell you what happened and you don't believe they've been at the same meeting? Well, I wondered whether these stakeholders lived on the same planet!

Interviewing the prime suspects

Let me give you the edited 'highlights'!

- The *operations department*'s problem was the design team – over-sensitive prima donnas who put services to their profession ahead of the customer. They didn't design things, they created monuments to their greatness. It was left to the operations department to agree practical changes with irate customers. Their solution was to incorporate design into operations.

- The *design department*'s problem was the customer-liaison department – who totally failed to manage customer expectations, leaving them asking for things they couldn't have, and the design team forced to play the bad guy and turn them down. Their solution was to incorporate customer-liaison into design.

- The *customer-liaison department*'s problem was the operations department – who tied them into using them for everything. The charges were astronomical and had to be passed on to complaining customers. Their solution was to outsource project delivery because managing contractors was easier than managing colleagues.

I also talked to front-line staff who'd lost confidence in their managers and to Steve's so-called project managers who saw their jobs solely as collecting information for progress reports. I didn't dare talk directly to customers but their comments on the customer feedback sheets told their sorry tale. Sound familiar?

And getting the whole story

I haven't gone into all the lovingly painted, expletive-deleted detail that my interviewees gave me but the fruits of our narrative rich discussions were all there in my notes.

> **Narrative-rich** discussions are where you basically get someone to tell you the whole story of the event. If they give you the little details, the nuances, their feelings [all the story's local colour] you can learn so much more about what's happening than you can with a 'just give me the hard facts' approach.

In the end, I'd amassed over thirty problems, which my intuition told me were connected in some way but which to the stakeholders were uniquely theirs.

Just call me Fox Mulder

I felt like Fox 'the truth is out there' Mulder from the *X Files* (but where was Scully when I needed her?). As I waded through my notes, I separated them into two categories:

- The undisputed facts of the situation – things (events) that were actually happening, that an independent observer could see and report back to other people.

- Conclusions people had come to on the basis of their interpretation of those facts – so I could see how each department interpreted the same events to create a totally different experience and a totally different problem.

> **Experience = event + interpretation**
> Very little of what we call our experience is things that happen to us [events]. Most of it is about how we interpret [make sense of] those events.

The events would give me a starting point for establishing common ground and the interpretations would give me clues as to what kind of solution would satisfy different stakeholders . . . if I ever got that far!

As I did this exercise, two common themes emerged. And because you've been there and got the T-shirt, there are no prizes for guessing what they were, so here they are.

We always blame someone else

According to each interviewee, the problem wasn't in their patch, it was in the other guy's; and they had the solution if only someone would listen. But each solution only favoured the department putting it forward so why should anyone listen? I understand that if you live in a blame-culture, you have to blame the other guy or you're admitting it was your fault but it was disheartening to learn that people had such big blindspots about the ways they were contributing to their own problems.

> The idea of a **blindspot** (the technical term is scotoma) has been borrowed by psychologists from the field of ophthalmology, where it means a situation in which part of a person's visual field just doesn't work. The person can see everything else, but they can see nothing in the area of the scotoma. And ▶

they cannot know what it is they aren't seeing. They are 'blind' to the 'blindspot'. In the field of psychology, it refers to a mental blindspot, where a person is simply unaware of their own role in creating a particular experience.

We can't see beyond our own problem

Talking of blindspots, they also didn't see that the other guy (a) might have a legitimately different perspective and (b) might feel justified in blaming them!

Our **perspective** is basically what we see from the position we are looking at things from. Anyone who is in a different position from you [including your team member] is bound to look at things differently. And as our actions are based on our interpretation of what we see and hear, a different perspective will lead to different action.

No, sir, their problem was *the* problem. I can see that up to a point – when I'm a customer with a problem; I don't care about the supplier's problems – but these people were supposed to be pulling together for the greater good of the customer and the organization.

Bracing myself for an uphill struggle

I concluded that people were focused on their own outputs rather than the outcomes of the project.

We produce **outputs** [things] to achieve **outcomes** [results]. The trouble is, we're often so focused on the outputs that we lose sight of the outcomes yet we exist to deliver outcomes not outputs. There are always more outcomes than you think and many are unintended. For example, if you're working with partners to develop a new product/service, there'll be an outcome about the quality of your relationship and, if you don't pay attention, it might not be an outcome you want.

Steve and I weren't going to be able to solve this problem by presenting them all with a neatly packaged solution. Half the battle would be to get them to see how their actions affected the other departments. And for that we needed to get them together to tell each other what they'd told me. Simple really!

IN SHORT

▶ **Everyone has a different problem.** Do you tend to focus more on the problem or the people having the problem?

▶ **It's easier to be the innocent victim.** Would your team say you have a tendency to blame other people when things go wrong?

▶ **Separate the events from people's experience of them.** Do you take people's interpretation of events as the truth?

6

Why is problem solving such hard work?

Emotions have to go somewhere, preferably somewhere productive

Fools rush in where angels fear to tread

I can't believe I was so naïve as to think it was just a matter of coming clean with each other but at the time I was in my 'logic rules, what's emotion got to do with it?' phase so, looking back, it does make a kind of sense.

And the reality doesn't live up to the dream

I didn't even get to first base. It wasn't hearing the head of the design department talk about 'our friends in operations' so much as the simpering smile he aimed at them while saying it. Who was this impostor and what had he done with the man who'd described that same colleague as a cowboy who wouldn't know a decent design if . . . the rest is unprintable. I tried to get them to talk about the real issues but, though anyone not in the know would have thought we were having a productive discussion, I knew avoidance when I saw it. About an hour passed, during which I was mentally counting the wasted cost in salaries of getting all these people together, before I decided it wasn't working. I called a five-minute comfort break and while they were out, I made copies of the notes I'd made on the undisputed facts.

Giving people no place to hide

When they got back, I said it might focus the discussion if everyone had a copy of my notes from the one-to-one meetings. As people started to read, the room fell into an oppressive silence. I smiled, thinking, 'Lucky you didn't see the unedited version'. I thought the neutral, non-blaming language would help people talk about the issues.

Talking of counting my chickens, we were still on item one when the arguments started and it wasn't long before it became a free for all. How many meetings have you been to where people, who were meant to come to a decision, just argued their proposal and only listened to other people to find the flaws in their proposal? At best it was going to end up like the heads of department meeting, with a package or pretty useless solutions, and at worst the rifts would take years to heal. I called a halt to the meeting and arranged another for the following week.

The trouble with structured problem-solving techniques

Next day, I sat down to work out what to do next. If we were going to get anywhere, we needed a structured problem-solving process. Over the years, I've tried more problem-solving techniques than I could write about in a book this size. You know the kind of thing, right? Force-field analysis, fishbone diagram, mind map, Delphi technique, affinity diagram, decision tree . . .

I've seen many a solution fail from lack of emotional ownership.

and so on. They work by distracting people away from cross-table arguing (an emotional state) and forward, usually towards a flip chart, into creative or analytical thinking (a cognitive state). That strength is also their weakness . . . because they only park the emotional issues associated with the problem, they don't solve them. I've seen many a solution fail from lack of emotional ownership. I needed a problem-solving process that allowed people to get the answer *and* process their emotions.

The old 'five whys' technique

I remembered a simple cause-and-effect technique I'd learned during my Total Quality Management days. It was called the 'five whys' – though I'm not sure why, as sometimes three were enough and sometimes it took a lot more than five. Enough to get people below the surface symptoms to the root-cause of a problem, I mean. I expect you've come across it before. It goes something like this.

There's a problem with water on the office floor. You could solve the symptom by having the floor mopped up but you ask why there's water on the floor. You discover there's a problem in the toilets on the floor above with an overflowing tap which means the symptomatic solution wouldn't have worked. You could solve this symptom by turning off the overflowing tap but you ask why the tap is overflowing . . . and so on until you discover a problem with the pipe that's causing washers to perish more quickly than they should. OK, not the most exciting example, but you get my drift.

With a bit of adaptation

Before I adapted the 'five whys', I did a review for learning on the previous meeting.

I regularly do **reviews for learning** with my team – sometimes one-to-one and sometimes with a whole project group, depending on the issue. We prepare by considering the following questions first on our own and then together.

- What went well and less well? What did I do to contribute to the outcome? What do I know now that I didn't know before?

- What have I learned about behaviour (about myself, the way other people behave etc.)? What insight have I gained about dealing with this kind of experience in the future?

- To enable me to use what I have learned what, if anything, do I need to challenge about the way I think or the way I behave? Are there any old ideas or behaviours I need to unlearn first?

- How, where and when can I use this insight to improve my performance?

I got two insights about the group.

- Because they only saw things from their perspective, they didn't see how their problem connected to the problems facing the people in the other departments so they ended up with symptomatic solutions.

- Because everyone had a different experience of the same event, they spent their time trying to persuade each other that their experience *was* the event, effectively invalidating the other person's experience; so there was a lot of inter-personal sensitivity attached to the problem now.

I thought I could expand the 'five whys' approach into a dia-gram showing the cause-and-effect relationship between the various problems. And if I made sure nothing went onto a problem statement without consensus that (a) it existed as an indisputable fact and (b) that the form of words describing it were acceptable to all, then the process of reaching that con-sensus would enable people to argue in a controlled way. And if I wrote up the problem statements on Post-it Notes and arranged them on a whiteboard, I could draw in the cause-and-effect links as we worked them out.

And some nifty facilitation

I thought about how to deal with the strong emotions that would inevitably surface. The trouble with anger is that it'll always come out (even if only in powerless forms like sulk-ing). But the textbook techniques for releasing emotions don't seem real to me. Maybe I've heard too many sarcastic stories from cynical colleagues about **Textbook techniques** touchy-feely, pseudo-psychotherapeu-**for releasing emotions** tic, hug-a-tree team-building week-**don't seem real.** ends. Or those 'Let's all get angry, act like children, say things any real man-ager will tell you are better left unsaid, then get over it' ses-sions with facilitators who open wounds they can't heal.

And I've never understood the logic of expressing your anger without the anger. Imagine the scene. A team member has dropped you in it, big time, and you're absolutely livid. You want his head on a plate and you're just about to indulge the temptation when, instead, you count to ten, sit down calmly and tell him in a suitably unemotional monotone that you're very angry. Well, maybe on a counsellor's planet but not on a real manager's!

On the other hand, humour – to be precise, taking something serious and emotionally tense and exaggerating it until it becomes ridiculous – is a great way of releasing tension through the belly-laugh that inevitably follows. Think about it. Laughter is as powerful an emotion as anger and the perfect safety valve in a heated situation. Sceptical? Have you ever been in a massive row, when, out of the blue, the other person says (or you think of) something unintentionally funny and all your anger instantly dissolves into hysterical laughter? Well, that's what I needed. A good problem-solving process and some heavy-duty laughter as a safety valve to release all those pent-up emotions.

IN SHORT

▶ **Channel argumentative people into emotionally productive tasks.** Have you ever experienced heated discussions that go nowhere except round in ever decreasing circles?

▶ **Choose problem-solving techniques that balance IQ and EQ.** What are your favourite problem-solving techniques and how well do they deal with the emotions underlying the problem?

▶ **Find a facilitation style that works for you.** What natural characteristics do you have that might help you shape your own approach to facilitation?

7

Why do we prefer to solve the wrong problem?

The comfort of the familiar versus the challenge of the root-cause

Dipping their toes in the water

At the next meeting, I ignored the list I'd given out previously but left it lying in the middle of the table as if to say 'Look, I know what the issues are, so don't pretend you haven't already told me'. And then I did a trainer trick for getting everyone involved – a round-robin. I went around the table asking each person in turn to describe their worst problem.

Then getting things off their chest

It was the longest, most tiring and yet fascinating round-robin I've ever done. As each person told the story of their worst problem, we got a real feel for what it was like for them. And giving them permission to get things off their chest in all the gory detail dissipated their anger. Then I asked them to summarize the problem in terms that were irrefutably observable and that the group would agree was fair. I don't think they could've done this before they'd released their emotions but, by this point, they were in the right frame of mind.

Their summary was, in effect, a draft problem statement, which we discussed until we reached an agreed form of words. Sometimes it felt like drafting a disarmament treaty between superpowers but whenever it got too heated I'd inject a bit of exaggeration and melodrama and get a laugh that released the tension. We always got to something we could genuinely agree on (all signs of pretence having long gone) and people didn't resent the neutral statements, perhaps because the same rule applied equally to everyone. Besides, we'd heard their story, so we all knew the emotion behind each statement. And agreement was something that hadn't happened for these people in years, so the more statements we agreed, the more confident they got about our ability to solve the problem. Because even the smallest successes will do that to people.

The more we agreed, the more confident they got.

And diving pretty deep

We unearthed all sorts of problems – logistics, managerial, financial, relationship and cultural. And when someone suggested that if you changed the subject you'd have the same problems in any big organizational system we all agreed. We may have been experiencing them in relation to the project-management issue, but the problems themselves were universal.

Once we'd got all the problem statements up on the whiteboard, I asked if anyone could see a cause-and-effect connection between any two of them. People offered up their intuitive connections and we challenged their logic until we arrived at a common-sense consensus. From this small beginning, we plugged away at making cause-and-effect chains between the various problem statements until the diagram grew more and more interconnected and we were forced to add new problem statements to complete some of the chains.

It was interesting to see how many problems people started to remember. My guess was they'd made up their minds as to the cause of the problems and their reticular activating system had ensured they didn't notice anything that might have provided counter-evidence.

Our **reticular activating system** [RAS] is a brain function that makes us notice things that are significant to us but not notice things that aren't. We need it because there's so much information to process all the time that without it we couldn't function. But guess which bit of the brain decides what we need and don't need to see? That's right, the subconscious!

But once I'd got them into an analytical exercise and they were looking at the cause-and-effect chains, logic showed them the missing pieces and the act of making the connections triggered things their subconscious had noticed but their conscious hadn't.

Before scurrying back to the comfort of the shallows

In total, we unearthed over forty-five problems (not surprising in a situation that had been going on for years) and we'd managed to track them all back to four causes. Which is where we hit the wall. As an observer, I could see a case for tracking three of those causes back to the fourth – the one describing the self-serving culture in each department. I'd been impressed to see that problem actually make it onto the whiteboard at all (they'd found it hard to admit to), so I wasn't surprised that they weren't ready to accept it might be the root-cause of over forty-five connected problems. I had to break through this last barrier but I couldn't see how. I called the meeting to a close and went away for another think.

There's a reason why root-causes are buried so deep

It was clear, from the discussion we'd had in writing up the problem statement, that they'd already judged self-serving as a bad thing. It was more comfortable to believe projects don't get delivered on time, within budget and to specification because of poor systems or unco-operative colleagues. But what if I could get them to look more neutrally at the self-serving thing? What if they chose to see it for what it is – a coping strategy, the best that people can do given the sense they've made of the situation they find themselves in?

> A **coping strategy** is a pattern of behaviour that we use repeatedly as a defence against things we fear we can't cope with. They're habits and, like everything else, can be helpful or hindering depending on the situation, the use you make of them and the effect they have.

Wherever you see a coping strategy that isn't working, you can bet fear isn't too far behind (because a coping strategy that's working will be producing a helpful effect not a problem). People weren't self-serving because they're bad people, they believed it was their only option for survival in what they saw as an organizational blame-culture. But it wasn't working . . . and I had to get them to stop judging themselves long enough to see that.

IN SHORT

▶ **Involve everyone in the problem-solving exercise.** How do you ensure everyone feels part of the process?

▶ **Face up to the real problems.** How often do you give in to the temptation of dealing with what you can see rather than what you know in your gut is really wrong?

▶ **And to your fears.** What stops you delving below the surface?

8

Why is the biggest problem what's in people's heads?

The real catalyst for problem solving is changing beliefs

People do what makes sense to them

I was ruthless at the next meeting. I challenged the logic of the proposed four root-causes and argued a series of cause-and-effect connections that left us with the self-serving culture as the only root-cause. They weren't very happy, I can tell you, but by then they were fully aware of the power of the cause-and-effect technique and couldn't argue with either the logic or the intuitive rightness of it.

Turning self-judgement into self-analysis

I chose to ignore the low spirits that overtook them at this point and asked them to identify the ways in which a self-serving culture could be hindering. They just pointed at all the problem statement Post-it Notes, which confirmed their acceptance of the root-cause. Then, because timing is crucial when you're challenging beliefs, I asked them to identify the ways in which a self-serving culture could be helpful. I had to push but eventually they came up with a number of ways and from there, it was a short hop to a consensus that it was understandable that people do what it takes to protect themselves, and that no one in their right mind would set themselves up to take the fall.

Exposing the core-conflict

They knew their coping strategy wasn't working from the problems they were having, so somewhere in the beliefs and behaviours associated with a self-serving culture was a core-conflict. It wasn't hard to find. Everyone believed on a conscious level that the self-interest of any department was best served by working together to deliver projects on time, within budget etc. Yet, the problem-solving process had surfaced their clear subconscious belief that the self-interest of each department was best served by 'looking after number one' and 'blaming the other guy'. And, in any conflict between our conscious and subconscious beliefs, our subconscious will always create the effects it wants, as it's stronger. Interestingly, what had been seen as an inter-departmental conflict was now seen as an internal conflict (between the conscious and subconscious of each person).

In any conflict between our conscious and subconscious beliefs, our subconscious will always create the effects it wants, as it's stronger.

And challenging the beliefs that underpin it

This is the moment when the hard slog of producing the cause-and-effect diagram, and the challenge of getting people to face the fact that they'd created the problem through their beliefs, pays off with a transformation of almost magical effect. All they needed to do was to make one last connection – the connection between the problems they'd created and the beliefs that underpin them – and challenge their validity.

Do you remember in Chapter 4 I told you that I hadn't experienced a blame-culture? In a controversial move, I told the group I thought their belief in a blame-culture had caused them to become self-serving, which in turn (in a self-fulfilling prophecy) had created a blame-culture. I said I could prove that the belief had come before the experience by telling a story from my own team. I didn't believe in blame and, though my team had been used to it, by acting in accordance with my belief, I'd changed what was in their heads. This had led to changes in their behaviour and, in time, the blame-culture had simply disappeared. I reminded them that they'd all blamed each other when we started but they didn't do it now, so they'd already started creating a new accountability-without-blame-culture. And that's the point of this step in the process – somewhere in the core-conflict behind every root-cause problem there's a belief that needs to be challenged, a belief that has created the root-cause problem in the first place.

To make the problem disappear

Problems are our subconscious telling us to challenge a hindering belief. Once they'd challenged their belief that there was a blame-culture, their belief that they needed to protect themselves from it went and the core-conflict disappeared. In a single, transformational meeting, their credo went from 'looking after number one' and 'blaming the other guy' to 'one for all and all for one' and 'accountability-without-blame', and the problem disappeared.

And to put something better in its place

After solving a twenty-year problem, the group were pretty fired up with enthusiasm and confidence. I didn't want it to evaporate, so I asked them to think about what their new credo would be like in real life, to describe what a neutral observer would see once it was in place by doing a 'walk-through'.

> A **walkthrough** is just when someone rehearses an event in their head by describing, in storytelling detail, what is happening from start to finish. It's a bit like doing a running radio commentary on a fantasy football match, if you'll pardon the metaphor. One person describes what's happening and the others ask questions to make sure no details get missed. You have to remember to keep asking questions of the 'where's the ref at this point?' kind, so you are sure nothing and no one gets missed. It sounds weird but it's great for anticipating potential problems.

Although I developed the 'walkthrough' as a way of anticipating problems on training events, it's also a good way to see how a new belief will work in practice.

From vision to reality

As each group member contributed to the 'walkthrough', I listed the key phrases they were using on a flip chart. Things like:

- Each department, manager and front-line employee is clear about their remit, responsibilities and roles, so no one treads on anyone else's toes.

- Everyone with a part to play in bringing a project to fruition attends regular inter-departmental project team meetings from the start of the project.

- As soon as someone spots a potential problem with a project they make sure everyone in the project team gets to hear about it quickly.

We didn't just get a clear picture of life under the new credo from this exercise, we got an action list for change – some action points were designed to address the 'root-cause' and others were 'symptomatic', to give compatible quick wins in individual problem areas.

And a plan to get from here to there

We developed the action list into an implementation plan. The problem-solving group decided to manage it themselves (they were now getting on as if they'd never been at war).

My last act as facilitator was to help them set up a radar system, so they had the feedback they needed to take appropriate action to sustain the new credo.

A **radar system** answers the question, 'What information do I need [in what form, at which points, after what triggers] to know if what is supposed to be happening is actually happening?' It's about giving you the feedback you need to intervene and take action either to put things back on track or change the track.

The process had taken time but we hadn't just achieved a fundamental breakthrough in solving the problem, we'd generated shared understanding across the departments and strong inter-departmental relationships that would serve us well in the future.

IN SHORT

▶ **Get people out of judging and into analyzing mode.** Do you fall into the trap of judging yourself harshly for things that in someone else you'd be more tolerant of?

▶ **Find the core-conflict in every problem.** Do you use problems as a way of challenging outdated beliefs?

▶ **Put something in place of the problem.** How do you react to 'problem solved'?

9

Why, even when I do everything right, does it still go wrong?

Because we're human beings, not robots – thank goodness!

What I learned from my problem-solving experience

I learned that if I'd been a better problem solver, I wouldn't have expected to be able to solve a twenty-year problem by discussion, so I'd have used a structured technique from the start. And if I'd known how hard it is for people to see how they create their own problems, I wouldn't have expected the members of the problem-solving group to be rational beings. I might have treated them more like the human beings they are.

Asking the tough questions

If we don't get the results we want, we have to face the possibility that we wanted our problem-solving attempts to fail. If so, we need to accept that, no matter how much we know logically (consciously) that we need to get down to the root-cause more often, our subconscious has an even stronger need for us to stay on the surface. And whatever the reason for that need, our subconscious will sabotage our efforts until we resolve the discrepancy. If your problem-solving attempts haven't worked as you would have liked, it may be because you fell into some of the same traps as I did. But before you start changing your approach, it's worth checking to see if you really do want to solve problems at their root-cause – by asking yourself . . .

What do I gain when problem solving goes wrong?

Do you get a buzz out of leaping into action at the first sign of a problem? Do you find it difficult to muster up the energy and the courage to face up to the real issues? I answered yes to these questions. Making the admission worth the effort means not self-judging but just accepting that human beings are complex – we do the best we can at the time to respond to our needs. It doesn't make us bad people, it just makes us human. But if we don't use what we've learned to move ourselves forward? Well, maybe that's when we should start beating ourselves up!

You already know everything you need to produce your best ever performance

Events happen, we interpret them to create an experience, then we store them in our subconscious. So why aren't we already effective? The reasons may be:

- The way we interpreted the event – which caused us to believe something that isn't realistic. Did we miss some of the lessons by only looking at it one way?

- We're only working with our conscious mind (our logic) – so we're not listening to our subconscious mind (our intuition). And if we're doing that, we aren't accessing all our experience in making our interpretation.

- We're only working with our subconscious – operating on autopilot and not using our conscious mind to check that what we're doing is logical. And if we're doing that, we're acting like children in situations that require us to act like adults.

The only way to be effective is to have your logic and intuition in balance . . . it's only common sense, after all.

Using this book to trigger your subconscious knowledge and insight

If people learn from experience, what's the point of reading a book? No point at all, if you don't make it into an experience. Remember:

Event + interpretation = experience

So if you just read the book, you've had an event, not an experience, and you won't learn anything from it. A good book will do three things:

- It will make you think, interpret and maybe challenge some of your beliefs and, in doing so, will become an 'experience' in its own right.

- It will bring to the surface things you already know on a subconscious level from your experience of life, so you can look more closely at them.

- It will expose you to someone else's experience so you can learn from that in the same way that you learn from your own experience and, in doing so, save yourself time and aggravation.

But it won't work if you read it on autopilot

I hope that as you read the rest of the book, you will pause every time something I say triggers either of the following responses:

- If you want to say, 'Well that's just common sense' – stop and ask yourself, 'Am I acting on what I know?' and 'Would other people be able to tell that's what I believe from the way I behave?'

- If you get an 'off' feeling – stop and work out what's making you feel like that. You don't have to agree with everything I say. My insight is only here to trigger yours – it's what makes sense to you that matters.

IN SHORT

- **We do what makes sense to us, so suspend self-judgement and look for your logic.** What do you have to gain when your problem-solving attempts go wrong?

- **If we're not as effective as we'd like to be, we need to reinterpret our experiences.** Looking back to your last experience of problem solving, what might a neutral observer say you'd missed?

- **A good book will trigger things your subconscious knows already.** What has made sense to you so far?

PART

2

■ *real* management for the way it is ■

Getting problem solving right in the _real_ world

▶ **Being too process-orientated gets us into more trouble than we know**

If you're anything like me, you've skipped straight to this page because it explains the problem-solving process from first throughts to final review for learning. Never mind telling me why it goes wrong, I hear you mutter, just tell me how to do it right. I wish I could but, sadly:

- Learning is about trial and error and the more you can learn from my trials and errors [in Part 1] the less time you need to waste doing your own.
- When it comes to getting results in the real world, you can't pin your faith on the kind of task-orientated processes that operate in most organizations. Why not? Because human beings have a habit of putting spanners in the works of even the best laid processes.

Process is important, I grant you [there's really no other way to get from start to finish in anything we do], but a process that's been designed without a proper understanding of what *can* go wrong, *will* go wrong.

How many times have you felt that you were serving a process that should be there to serve you? On my good days I see process as a necessary evil and on my bad days it's the enemy that makes me manage like a robot. And speaking of enemies, I like the martial arts idea of deflecting your opponent's strength against itself, so I design inclusive processes that take account of all the things that normal processes leave out, things that make me more people-orientated.

▶ It's not my process that matters – it's yours

Most management writers will tell you, 'Follow this process and you'll be fine'. I only wish it was true. But the truth is, no one but you can know what it's like in your world, so no one but you can design a problem-solving process that works for you. What I can do is describe seven generic steps that will identify all the things you need to think about when you're designing your own problem-solving process. So, as you read through each step, remember the insights you got from reading Part 1, and think about how you can use the process to help you address those issues.

10

How do you know you're working on the right problem?

Understanding all the problem variables so you can manage the dynamic

A weed is a flower in the wrong place

That's all I remember from a horticulture course I started but never finished (too much digging, too many worms) but it was a transformational thought. And, no, not just because I now look at lawns full of daisies in a whole new light but because it gave me the definition of a problem.

A problem is just an unwanted effect

Think about it. If the same flower that's admired on a woodland walk is denounced as a weed in a cultivated border, then it follows that whatever is happening is only a problem if it's unwanted. I'm reminded of a woman I know whose garden-loving husband causes her a problem by traipsing mud into the house. I also know an elderly woman living alone with a large rambling garden who'd like nothing better than someone who traipsed mud into the house while restoring her garden to its former glory. Is a muddy floor a problem? Depends whose floor it is.

Effect + negative interpretation = problem

In Chapter 2, I said that if you weren't happy with the effects you were creating (in other words, if you have problems), one of your choices was 'reframing' – reinterpreting the effect so it becomes positive not negative (and is therefore no longer a problem). I can't tell you how many problems my staff have brought to me over the years that I've made disappear just by getting them to think about how they could turn it to their advantage. And no, that doesn't make me a manager who says, 'Don't bring me problems, bring me solutions'. I'm solution-focused not simple-minded.

We're hard-wired to solve problems

Our subconscious defines a problem as any variation from the norm. It registers a variation whenever something isn't happening that should be, or is happening that shouldn't be. It's a throwback to the days when survival depended on our ability to solve potentially life-threatening problems, when interpreting any variation from the norm as a problem was a very helpful bit of hard-wiring. But, in the modern world, despite its many dangers, we're not often faced with the kind of life or death problems that our ancestors faced on a daily basis. Yet that survival instinct still manifests itself in the way we're driven to keep our problem-solving abilities sharp. Why else are we attracted to everything from puzzle books and crosswords to quiz shows and action adventure films, where if we don't get to see the star solve a seemingly insoluble problem, the film is a big disappointment?

But who is 'norm'?

You know the song 'Big Yellow Taxi' – written and sung by Joni Mitchell but maybe more familiar to some readers from Amy Grant's cover version? I used to think that line about not knowing what you've got till it's gone was just a salutary reminder about not taking things for granted. Now I think it's telling us to surface our norms before it's too late. Norms are expectations about how things should be that we often don't realize we have until things change.

> **Subconscious expectations** are pre-programmes that tell us what to expect in certain situations or with certain people.

So, we may, for instance, be unaware of our expectation to see trees in towns until one day we find they've been cut down to make way for 'parking lots'. In defining a problem as 'an unwanted effect' there's an assumption that we're conscious of what would be an unwanted effect. But life isn't that simple, as you'll know if you've ever experienced not knowing what you wanted until you didn't get it (or not knowing what you didn't want until you did). Those are the kinds of situations that bring our subconscious expectations rushing into our conscious.

And when expectations are subconscious, we aren't prompted to check whether they're realistic, which can also cause problems. Am I alone in thinking I've got a problem when an employee won't work late because, unlike me, he has a life? It's easier for me to challenge my unrealistic expectation than try to solve that kind of 'problem', I can tell you. I almost daren't tell you this (you'll think I'm sad) but I like problems because when I surface and challenge my subconscious expectations I learn a lot about myself.

Changing our 'norms' is one way of making problems disappear

Knowing all this, we can make many of our problems disappear just by surfacing and challenging our subconscious expectations. Neat trick, eh! Here's how it works. A team member stomps into my office, plonks down in the chair, composes his face into a curmudgeonly expression and moans about some managers who were supposed to attend today's course who hadn't turned up, or had the courtesy to let him know beforehand. He's pretty worked up and I don't blame him – he put a lot of effort into putting on a good course and it's a bummer when people don't show, not to mention a waste of a very expensive trainer who charges full-rate whether people show or not. But it's a commonplace occurrence and I'm surprised by his reaction. So I say, 'Well, what did you expect? Full attendance except for those who've given you prior warning of their absence?'. I give him my 'Hello, what planet do you live on?' look and he sees his subconscious expectation for what it is – unrealistic. He changes it to something more realistic and he no longer has a problem. He just has an event that got 90 per cent attendance instead of 100 per cent, which is actually pretty good by industry standards.

But what about the *real* problems?

Let's assume you've surfaced your subconscious expectations and they survived the 'two Rs' (realistic and reasonable) challenge. And let's assume you've made several attempts to reframe the event in question and, though you can now see one or two potential upsides, you still think there's a problem. Well, then you need to look at the problem's variables so you can manage them. Let's have a look at them.

Problems, like people, have characteristics

Think about a problem you're dealing with at the moment. What are its characteristics? Is there just one unwanted effect or a number of them? Does it affect just you or other people? Does it affect everyone in the same way or in different ways? Is there anyone who's actually benefiting from the problem – who sees the effects as wanted and who might sabotage solutions in the hope of maintaining the status quo? Is it complicated or simple? Is it within your own control to solve or does it need input from other people? Does it stand in isolation or is it part of a number of interlinked problems? Is there just one right answer or many possible solutions? Is it a long-term or short-term problem? Is it high-risk or low-risk? Now think about another problem you're dealing with at the moment and ask yourself the same set of questions. Different answers? Well, every problem is different.

You're a variable too

What's your attitude to problems? Do you live in denial until you've no choice but to face them, or do you prefer to confront every little thing before it becomes a problem? Are you a *Krypton Factor* junkie who thrives on a challenge, or do you sigh deeply and long for a quiet life? One person's idea of a stress-free life is another person's idea of boredom. Even people who get a buzz out of solving problems react to some problems differently from others, leaping with unbridled enthusiasm into the most intellectually exhausting problems, but running a mile from the tiniest people problem.

One person's idea of a stress-free life is another person's idea of boredom.

Your problem-solving style also affects how you approach problems and how people approach you with their problems. Do you like to start with the big picture and then work down to the small print, or do you prefer to start small and build up? Do you notice the people aspects of the problem first or the technical aspects? Are you more Mr Spock (logical) or Captain Kirk (intuitive)? Do you prefer solutions that are fair and equitable or that everyone is happy with? No two people will solve the same problem in the same way.

No one ever solved a problem in a vacuum

Let's go back to the idea of a weed being a flower in the wrong place and think about the impact of place. Think about places where you've worked and their operating contexts.

Operating context includes anything or anyone in your organizational or external environment that affects performance. Primarily that means people [customers, suppliers, colleagues, staff and stakeholders], your organizational culture and the external factors affecting your organization.

Have you ever done something in one organization that would have caused a problem if you'd done it in another? Is your organization highly structured or fairly loose? If it has rules (norms) for even the smallest things, it will inevitably have more instances of variations and so more problems. Is your organization controlling or empowering? Are people allowed to solve their own problems or expected to pass them up the line? How are you fixed for resources – do people throw money at problems or don't you get the resources you need to pursue innovative solutions? I'm being either/or here when in real life it's a continuum, but you get my point. No organization is either all 'can-do' or all 'can't-do' but you can bet there are more problems, that are harder to solve, in the places the 'can-do' culture hasn't reached.

Where do you fit into the organization? How does your position affect the way you solve problems? Do you have the power you need to put solutions in place, or do you need to get approval at a higher level? Overall, how does your organization view problems – as opportunities for innovation or disruptions to their steady state?

Problems have a history and change over time

Who said if we don't learn from the past we're doomed to repeat it? By the sound of it, they knew the history of a problem has an effect on its dynamic. Previous attempts to solve the problem will have changed the way the problem now appears, not necessarily for the better, as Steve's problem in Part 1 shows. And as you engage with a problem, the passing of time will change your perspective on it, so try to keep an open mind and remember that your first solution isn't the only solution.

Who else is involved?

Although you may be the only person affected in a particular way, it's unlikely you're the only person affected. Other stakeholders in the problem are a variable that needs to be managed. That problem you were thinking about earlier? Who else has an interest in it, or an impact on either the problem or your ability to solve it? The next chapter is devoted to stakeholders, as they're crucial both to getting a clear picture of the problem in its many guises and to getting ownership of the solution, so I won't pre-empt it here.

It's the interplay of the variables that creates the dynamic

The nature of the problem, its history, the characteristics of the problem solver, the organizational context within which the problem exists and the different stakeholders affected by the problem all come together to create a unique dynamic that you need to understand to achieve a solution.

Managing the complexity to get to the simplicity

When it comes to 'problems' we chose, such as overcoming obstacles to fulfil a cherished ambition and we engage with the problem on conscious and subconscious levels, we see just how good we are at solving problems. But at work there are too many problems so we want quick fixes – we don't want to engage with them. Yet, if you do engage with a problem and solve it at root-cause level, there's a gratifying domino effect, that solves all the spin-off problems at the same time. And, for me, there's a compelling simplicity in that. You don't have to engage with *all* your problems, only with the one that makes the others disappear.

> **If you engage with a problem and solve it at root-cause level that solves all the spin-off problems at the same time.**

IN SHORT

▶ **We choose our problems.** What do you think your problems would tell an unbiased observer about you?

▶ **Thinking differently can make problems disappear.** Have you ever found yourself changing your perspective so that a problem no longer felt like a problem?

▶ **No two problems are the same.** When you compare your work problems, which do you see more easily – the similarities or the differences?

11

How do you ensure you're seeing the problem from all the angles?

Understanding the stakeholders' problems and needs

Every stakeholder's problem is different

Pardon the cliché but I have a friend with a problem. She never sees her workaholic husband. She lives in a rural area and doesn't drive so she's at home on her own all day. And when he does come home all he wants to do is vegetate in front of the television. Her husband has a different problem. He loves his job, gets so absorbed in a task that he doesn't notice how late it is and when he gets home he just wants to unwind in peace and quiet and not be faced with a clingy, dependent wife who wants to break her day's silence.

Event plus interpretation equals experience. The husband and wife would agree on the events – he works late, she is alone all day, she doesn't drive and so on – but they create completely different experiences of those events. As outside observers, we might say *they* have *a* problem but we're relating to the events (which are shared) not the experience (which isn't). And we can do that (take an objective viewpoint) because it's not *our* problem. But they can't because to

Stakeholders don't just have a different perspective, they have a different problem. them it's personal. And that's the most important thing when you're working with stakeholders. Stakeholders don't just have a different perspective, they have a different problem. And it won't help if you merge everything into one generic problem because that only serves to invalidate stakeholders' problems.

You *will* need to see the connections – but not yet

With the main theme of this book being connecting problems to get to the root-cause, I must sound like I'm contradicting myself here. But solving a problem has two major elements: one is getting to the root-cause so you can deal with it at source and the other is managing the people, because no matter how ingenious your solution, if the stakeholders don't like it, it won't happen. The problem-solving method in this book achieves both separateness and connection in the same cause-and-effect technique (more on that in Chapter 13). But in this chapter, I'm focusing on getting a clear understanding of the experiences of different stakeholders so you need to be self-disciplined about not forming premature conclusions about connections and root-causes and the like.

Finding the problem's stakeholders

I wish I could give you a simple, structured way of doing this but the reality is it's a haphazard affair. You can start by listing all the individuals/groups you *think* are affected by the problem (been there, done that, thought I had it cracked) but be warned that once you start talking to people, you can bet they'll tell you about someone else (or indeed several some-ones) you need to speak to as well. So, ignore the worry that you're on a wild-goose chase and follow the trail wherever it takes you so you can experience by proxy the problems of as many of the stakeholder groups as possible.

If you *can* ask stakeholders, *do* ask them

The simplest way of learning about someone's problem is to ask them. Assuming, for the moment, that asking them is a viable proposition (we'll come shortly to what you can do if it's not), get them to tell you their story in narrative-rich form. Don't forget to:

- *Listen without judging* – you're trying to understand their experience of the problem. It will be different to yours and you want to dispute it but this isn't the time or place. If you're judgemental now you won't build the relationship you need for later.

- *Gently steer them into neutral* – at first they'll only be able to see it the way they always have. By asking exploratory, non-judgemental questions, you can get them to think about any potential upsides to the problem. Tread carefully (you don't want them to become defensive) but get them away from judging, towards analyzing.

- *Expect them to give you their solutions* – but bear in mind if they aren't experts they'll only have a limited idea of the range of possibilities. And I know I told *you* not to think about solutions at this stage, but move *them* do it. It gives you clues about what's important to them, which will help you generate solutions they'll like.

- *Accept their judgements and interpretations for what they are* – their experience, not an objective description of events, and explore the underpinning beliefs. Again, this will tell you what's important to them.

- *Get as much clarity as you can* – about what they've observed as well as their interpretations. For example, if a stake-holder who's an internal customer says, 'They (the supplying department) deliberately ignored what I wanted' make a note of that then ask, 'What did they actually do to make you come to that conclusion?'.

- *Look out for counter-evidence* – anything that jars with their overall assessment. When people make their minds up about what the problem is, their reticular activating system won't let them see anything that doesn't fit, but you will notice it.

But what if you can't ask them?

It's not always possible or sensible to ask some stakeholders about their perspective on a problem. You might not want customers to know there *is* a problem. And even if you do, going public is also telling your competitors. So, think carefully about who you talk to . . . but, of course, don't let it stop you finding out what their perspective and needs are. Just use a different method.

Like most things to do with human nature, our **needs** are simultaneously complex and simple. Simple because we only have two core needs – avoid pain and get pleasure [or, as we get older and more sophisticated, to avoid negative consequences and seek positive consequences]. Complex because our beliefs about what causes pain and pleasure are unique to us.

Empathy is an overrated skill

We hear a lot about empathy these days as it's a big component of emotional intelligence, or EQ as it's come to be known, in juxtaposition to IQ (cognitive intelligence). Contrary to popular belief, empathy is the ability to understand how someone else experiences an event and not about how *you* would experience it in their shoes.

> I prefer **imagination** to **empathy** because empathy is so easy to get wrong. Too often people think empathy is about how we'd feel if we were in someone else's situation. But we get it wrong because we take our own frame of reference with us whereas, if we actually were in their situation, we'd be looking from a different perspective, so we'd feel and do things differently. Getting this wrong is often what stops us understanding people.

The people we describe as empathic are often sympathetic – compassionate people who wrap us in the comfort blanket of their supportive response, making us feel all warm and fuzzy – it's nice but not the same thing at all. But the goal of empathizing is not to make the other person feel good, it's to achieve real understanding. And you don't have to feel an emotional connection to someone or agree with their point of view to achieve that.

The goal of empathizing is not to make the other person feel good, it's to achieve real understanding.

It goes against our hard-wiring

We each have our unique way of looking at the world (our frame of reference) that helps us make sense of our day-to-day experiences. Our subconscious is attached to our frame of reference, keeping us sane by making the external world match it, yet empathizing asks us to put aside our frame of reference and take on someone else's. And it's hard work. A friend told me she was going into hospital for a routine operation. My frame of reference about hospitals includes a phobia about operations so I immediately 'empathized' based on how I would feel in her situation. I reassured her that it needn't be a nightmare only to discover that her frame of reference about hospitals included being waited on hand and foot, getting lots of rest and a complete break from the demands of her daily life. Oh dear. My reassurances were not only unempathic, they actually put thoughts into her head that left her more worried at the end of the conversation than she'd been at the start.

The amazing imagination-for-empathy technique

As you can see, I've never really gotten the hang of empathy, but to be honest I hope I never do, because the technique I use at work gets better results. It's simple and doesn't leave you feeling the emotional equivalent of a wet teabag. It's a four-step process:

1. Brainstorm all the ways of interpreting the event/situation. One interpretation will come naturally to you (that's the one that's based on your own frame of reference) but try to identify as many different interpretations as possible.

2. Think about the person you're trying to identify with. What are they like? How do they react in other situations? What do you know from your experience of them?

3. Go back to the list from step 1 and select the interpretation that best fits what you know about them. This won't

necessarily be the one that makes the most sense to you but it *will* be one you think would make the most sense to them.

4. Find a way of checking whether you're right. The easiest way is to tell them what you were thinking and ask them if you're on the right lines. But if you can't do that, work out how they'd react if that *was* their interpretation then see if they do react that way, as that will confirm your understanding.

If you get a long enough list for step 1, you can use it for each stakeholder group. Just start at step 2 for each group in turn and select the most appropriate interpretation.

And why do I call it the *amazing* imagination-for-empathy technique? Because sometimes, that's all it takes to make the problem disappear. I'm still proud of the fact that ten years ago I used it to help save the marriage of a contractor who was doing some work on my house. He was at his wits' end about a problem he'd had for years with his wife. I offered him several alternative interpretations (step 1), helped him work out which was the most likely (steps 2 and 3) which wasn't the one he'd previously thought. He did step 4 himself, then tried a different response based on his new interpretation, created a different experience and got his marriage back on track. Amazing or what!

And so versatile too

If that's not enough, it's the perfect preparation for designing a questionnaire or survey because all you have to do is pick out the most likely interpretations and put them into multiple-choice format. And you can use it as prompts for discussion when facilitating focus groups.

What's more, you can use it to get behind the way people experience a problem to their beliefs and needs. You start with the outcome from step 4 – the interpretation most likely to reflect a particular stakeholder group – and then you do step 1 again. But this time, you brainstorm what they might have to believe in order to interpret the event that way. From the list of possible beliefs, think about what you know about them (step 2), select the belief that seems to fit them best (step 3) and check your understanding (step 4).

Knowing what's what and who's who

If you've tackled the process of understanding the perspective of the problem's stakeholders effectively, you'll have reached the end of this step with a lot of information about both the problems and the people affected by them. Now all you have to do is use what you've learned to help you engage with the problem and watch the answer appear as if by magic! But first, let's make sure you're not the only one doing that.

IN SHORT

- **Problems need to be separated and connected.** Which do you tend to see more readily – the separateness of your problems or the connectedness?

- **Empathy is a high-risk strategy.** Have you ever had an attempt at empathizing go wrong?

- **Imagination works better than empathy.** How often do you use your imagination at work?

12

How do you ensure everyone affected by the problem takes appropriate responsibility?

Establishing and managing a problem-solving group

From a child's approach to problem solving

Last year I signed up for a weekly series of one-hour one-to-one yoga lessons. The first started on time but each week we seemed to start a bit later. I had to be somewhere else immediately afterwards, so I couldn't overrun to make up my full hour, but I made allowances anyway. Eventually, when it got to the stage where I was losing a quarter of my lesson time, I said something. By then, of course, I had the kind of pent-up frustration that defeated the object of the lesson and contributed to my sounding suspiciously like a sulky child instead of an adult who had a right to get what she'd paid for. My teacher was surprised by my reaction because he'd just assumed I was relaxed about the situation. He went on to say (in an equally sulky tone) that if I'd mentioned it earlier, he'd have made sure he finished his previous lesson on time – which left me feeling I'd caused the problem! Both my teacher

ALLOCATING RESPONSIBILITY

and I had acted like children, neither taking responsibility for the situation. I'd recognized my problem but not done anything about it, and he was in denial about his problem of not giving the customer what the customer had paid for.

To an adult's approach

Problems often arise because we haven't set clear boundaries with people about what's acceptable and what's not. This can be for selfish reasons (when we want to keep the peace or only have the energy for the line of least resistance) and/or unselfish reasons (when we want to show someone that we accept them for who they are, warts and all). But, whatever the reasons, our acceptance of a problem is saying to the person causing the problem that it's okay for them to continue. And that's not a caring act because you may be helping them in the short term (by colluding with their avoidance issue) but you aren't helping them in the long term. Because ultimately their approach will create negative experiences for them and they won't thank you for not helping them when it was smaller and more manageable. That's right, we save people from the consequences of their experience at our peril as well as theirs.

> **Our acceptance of a problem is saying to the person causing the problem that it's okay for them to continue.**

You know we all learn by trial and error using feedback.

By **feedback**, I mean any signs we pick up about reactions to what we're doing. It's not just the formal feedback we get when the boss reviews our work, it's all the little signals we don't necessarily notice consciously but that our subconscious picks up and uses to adjust our thinking, behaviour and actions. We get feedback all the time, regardless of whether we think we do. Without it, we'd never know how to adjust course to achieve our intentions.

77

By staying silent we give people the wrong feedback, because without negative consequences they'll continue to believe they're doing the right thing, and so won't challenge their beliefs. Be an adult and sweat the small stuff, I say, then the big stuff won't happen.

But beware the temptation of being a parent

It's not just when we act like children that we're failing to act like responsible adults. I worked with someone who enjoyed her reputation as a problem solver, who was always there for a friend in need and (no surprises here) they were often in need. The day she saw the light was when she was telling me about a friend who'd applied for a job for which she had to do a presentation. My team member had 'helped' her with it. I put the word in inverted commas because a more accurate description would be that she had done it for her. Her friend got the job, which should have been a happy ending, but it wasn't. She turned the job down because she didn't feel confident in her ability to do it. And why not? Because she hadn't been responsible for producing the presentation that had secured the job offer. Parental helping doesn't help.

Matching responsibility to power . . . not just authority

You've already identified the stakeholders and learned about their experience of the events they're interpreting as problems. You'll be using that information at two points in the problem-solving process – this is the first one.

Think about how much power each stakeholder (stakeholder group) has. Don't assume only managers have the authority to solve problems. Yes, hierarchy does give managers authority but ask any manager who's tried to implement change against the wishes of the front-line and you'll see that authority isn't real power. Authority is the organizational perpetuation of the parent/child relationship and, as any parent knows, the child can and often does rebel against that authority (whether overtly or covertly). Think about the people who hold real power through their role model influence on their peer group and/or the respect they have gained at all levels for their knowledge and expertise. The problem-solving process in this book starts from the belief that every employee has the power to solve all sorts of problems, even those that at first sight seem beyond their capability and authority. This stage of the process is about getting them to see and accept that.

When you're thinking about stakeholders, divide them into two types:

- *Impact groups* – are people who can affect the outcome of the problem-solving process. It will include senior managers who need to approve changes or allocate resources, but it also includes people who can sabotage (either consciously or subconsciously) the solution. These people need to be in the problem-solving group.

- *Interest groups* – are people who can't affect the outcome of the problem-solving process but who may have an insight into its cause or an idea for a solution. They don't need to be in the problem-solving group but they *do* need to be consulted.

Once you've have identified the members of the problem-solving group, you need to agree separately with each one (before you bring them together) their specific responsibilities. Psychologists warn us about a number of difficulties facing groups working together and this is designed to prevent them. Two of the biggest are 'diffusion of responsibility' where people take less responsibility for a problem in a group than they do on their own, and 'group-think' where people get carried away to greater extremes than they would on their own. Obviously, what you allocate to whom will depend on the problem, but here are some potential responsibilities:

- *To the problem-solving group* – for challenging assumptions and keeping the problem-solving process clean.
- *To the interest groups* – for gathering input from them.
- *To the system in which the problem exists* – for what happens in their parts of it.
- *To the problem* – for their contribution to the problem.
- *To the solution* – for implementing it within their specific sphere of influence.

A problem-solving group or a virtual reference group – it's your choice

I'm focusing here on a problem-solving process that involves people but if circumstances are against an involving approach, you can set up a virtual reference group made up of stakeholders who you can 'work' with using the 'imagination-for-empathy' technique.

Your responsibility – managing the problem-solving group

As facilitator, you're responsible for managing the performance of the problem-solving group – and I do mean managing, which means three things:

- *Managing their performance* – all the things you'd do for a member of your own team, including holding them accountable for their actions and inactions. Yes, I know they have a line manager who manages them in their day job, but what does their line manager know about their performance in the problem-solving group?

- *Developing their performance* – being on the lookout for hindering beliefs that affect the group members, so you can coach them to a better contribution. Yes, I know tradition says it's the line manager's job but the new rules of EQ say we all have a responsibility to help each other do the best we can.

- *Empowering their performance* – helping them tap into the power they already have, so they don't play the victim in their own melodrama. I don't have to tell you the difference a 'can-do' attitude can make.

And ensuring the problem-solving process works

You need to ensure no one ducks the issues – no mean feat as, let's face it, if people had done that in the past, you wouldn't have a problem now. To do it you need to develop a facilitation style that works with your characteristics but, as a starter for ten, let me tell you what works for me. I'm a sensitive soul, prone to what other people see as over-reactions – they're totally, utterly, completely and absolutely wrong, of course. I used to think of my sensitivity as a weakness but since I started applying the idea of characteristics, I've found ways of turning it to my advantage. I use it to pick up potential sensitivities before they turn into inter-personal problems. I also (I might as well tell you while I'm in confessing mode) have a drama

Develop a facilitation style that works with your characteristics.

I guess even the most sceptical of us would accept that different relationships and different situations bring out **different 'sides' to our character**. I like to think of the 'sides' of my character as characters in their own right because it helps me keep a sense of humour and be less self-critical when I do something daft. Each of your cast of characters represents a need that won't go away just because you ignore it and is often associated with a cluster of characteristics you don't use any other time.

queen in me who enjoys being the centre of attention – had you guessed that already?

I let my drama queen out when I can feel tension brewing. Picture me clutching my heart or holding my head in my hands and saying, 'Crikey Fred, it's lucky John isn't sensitive. I'd have been sulking for England by now if you'd said that to me'. By exaggerating the point to its extreme I'm not only getting a laugh, I'm speaking straight to the subconscious of the 'perpetrator'. They don't recognize it as negative feedback on a conscious level but their subconscious does and their behaviour changes. It also allows the 'victim' to say it hadn't bothered them (whether it had or not). It gets the negative feedback job done and cuts the tension and, if I say so myself, I'm getting pretty skilled at the whole laughing-at-people-till-they-laugh-at-themselves thing.

You're **skilled** when you can consistently produce your desired effect. Some people would argue that if you make someone feel snubbed, for example, you do not have good inter-personal skills. I say that if that's what you intended, then you're skilled and if it's not what you intended, you're not.

Of course, not everyone is an over-sensitive budding-comic, ham-acting exaggerator, so if you can't in a million years picture that, try the safety-in-numbers approach. Get everyone to agree some rules up front, then put them on 'dialogue alert' so everyone polices each other. What's 'dialogue alert' I hear you ask? Well, let me explain what dialogue is first because it's a much maligned term.

And that dialogue rules, okay

Dialogue happens when everyone is genuinely interested in what everyone else has to say and where they're coming from and where the point of listening is to understand not to find the weakness in their position so you can win the argument. It requires three things:

- *Equality* – everyone leaves their position and authority level at the door and treats each other as people who have things of equal value to bring to the problem.

- *Suspending judgement* – being in 'explore mode' when listening to people and understanding that everyone has a right to interpret events however they want when creating their experience.

- *Surfacing assumptions and beliefs* – where everyone is on the lookout for hindering beliefs and brings them to the attention of the group so they can be challenged.

In being on the alert for breaches of the dialogue rules, you'll all be working together to create an atmosphere of mutual respect. And before you dismiss respect as a given, count how many times you hear people start their sentences with the words 'with all due respect' only to follow it up with a complete lack of respect.

By asking a lot of questions

You should expect different stakeholders to have different perspectives on the same issue because it's a pluralist world out there. So, when you hear one perspective, ask for others (but don't imply one perspective is more valid than another). Listen out for the minority view, try assuming it can shed light on the problem (it always does in my experience) and ask questions to probe it. Many people find it hard to stand out from the crowd and aren't always at their most articulate when offering a dissenting voice so try to listen to what lies behind the words and ask questions to get clarity.

This is an ongoing task

Sorry to end with a health warning but I know what us linear types can be like. You can't just do this step in the process and think that's it – responsibility established. You need to be on constant alert for signs of 'backsliding' and be ready to reprise the ideas in this chapter whenever they're needed.

IN SHORT

▶ **Take an adult approach to problem solving.** Would an unbiased observer describe you as a child, parent or adult in the way you deal with your problems?

▶ **Find people's real power and charge them with using it.** Do you ever fall into the trap of underestimating what you and others are capable of achieving?

▶ **Get a genuine dialogue going.** Is there ever a sense of real equality in the exchanges between people at different levels in your organization?

13

How do you get to the bottom of what's wrong?

Establishing the cause-and-effect chain and exposing the core-conflict

Preparing for the cause-and-effect exercise

In Chapter 11, you got information from the stakeholders on their experience of the problems. In Chapter 12, you used it to sort out the responsibilities of the different stakeholders. Now you use it again, to prepare for the 'cause-and-effect' exercise. When you look at your notes you'll probably see that people talked about seemingly unrelated issues – you may even have got the 'everything but the kitchen sink' response. Don't be tempted to prune it back – trust that the connections are there, just on a subconscious level.

Trust that the connections are there, just on a subconscious level.

You'll probably also notice that information came across in a mishmash of observations, interpretations, experience, events, speculations and blame, so you need to disentangle and 'neutralize' it.

Having wished I hadn't circulated the notes in advance in Part 1, I'm now a fan of doing it provided you also do the round-robin exercise so you're not relying on people having ownership of what is, in essence, an outside observer's write-up of the problems. But you know your stakeholders better than me, so decide what to do each time on the merits of the case. If you don't circulate them, they're still an excellent aid to your facilitation.

Starting the ball rolling

I recommend you use a whiteboard and Post-it Notes for the 'cause-and-effect' exercise. Write each problem on a separate Post-it Note and as you build the cause-and-effect connections, stick them to the whiteboard and use a marker pen to draw an arrow between the problem statements in the direction of the cause-and-effect relationship. Get the first batch of problem statements by going round the group and asking each person at a time to identify the worst problem from their perspective. Apart from closing the psychological loop-hole that allows people to avoid taking ownership, the benefits are:

- You all gain an insight into what each person's biggest problem is.

- People get things off their chests, which clears the air for the rest of the task. Go round the room as many times as you need to.

- It acts as an ice-breaker (believe it or not) because everyone has to take part.

- You can work out which members of the group are not as forthcoming in front of their colleagues as they were in the one to one.

- Because you're treating everyone's problem as equally important, it reinforces the principles of dialogue and sets the tone for what's to come.

Make sure the problem statements are written up properly

Although people can say anything they like when describing their problem, what actually gets written up on the Post-it must be in neutral language. It must reflect what's actually been observed in real life (the event) rather than the interpretation made by the various different observers (experience). Also, the problem statement must be agreed and have a shared understanding (don't assume it, check) among the group. Finally, because almost every problem statement both causes a higher level problem and is caused by a lower level problem, allow only one problem statement per Post-it Note and no implied causes. All this sounds (and often is) long-winded but the ownership it generates and the chances it offers for people to release their emotions, understand each other and build relationships pay massive dividends. Depending on how many people you're working with and how many times you went round the table, you may well have a fair few Post-it Notes stuck to the whiteboard, but I can guarantee you that you won't have them all!

Finding the cause-and-effect relationships between the problems

The next stage is to ask the group to look at all the problem statements and see if they can suggest whether any one is the cause of any other. So, if one problem is staff shortages in the team and another is that customers don't get their products on time, someone might suggest that the former is the cause of the latter. As people are using their intuition to make these connections, and as you want a common-sense result, you need to make sure the connections are also logical by asking questions like:

- *Does the first problem have to happen to get the second problem?* Are there reasons, other than staff shortages, why customers don't get their products on time?

- *Is the first problem sufficient on its own to cause the second problem?* Do other things (apart from staff shortages) cause bottlenecks, such as receiving a higher than normal number of orders?

- *Does the first problem cause problems other than the second problem?* Does the short-staffing also cause pressure in the team and does that then cause a higher than normal number of errors? This question may lead you to connect with a problem that's already on a Post-it Note but it may also lead you to add a new one.

Look out for more problems

Once you've established one cause-and-effect connection, keep asking people to offer suggestions for more connections until you're satisfied that you've joined up all the problems. If you've got good spatial awareness you'll end up with a beautiful hierarchical diagram that shows surface-level, symptomatic problems at the top and a single root-cause problem at the bottom, from which all the other problems stem. However, if you're like me, you'll have something that would win the Turner Prize, so you'll have to tidy it up a bit before showing it outside the group. If you look closely, you'll see how the surface-level problems at the top of the diagram link back into the root-cause problem via a reinforcing loop that's what caused the whole mess to sustain itself . . . well, you didn't think it was your fault that it'd gone on for years, did you? As you work through this process, you need to remember the challenge process will generate problem statements that didn't come up when you first went round the table. Before you write them up, subject them to the same rules and tests that you applied to the original problem statements.

Knowing when you've got to the root-cause

How do you know when you've got to the root-cause problem? It can be when you can track every problem on the whiteboard back through the connecting arrows to a single Post-it Note. It can be when you look at your potentially root-cause problem and realize the next level down is a belief rather than an observable effect. To be honest though, it's more likely you'll know because everything will just click into place.

Pause to look at what the cause-and-effect diagram is telling you

'Why pause?', I hear the cynics asking, as if enjoying the moment isn't enough justification. And I can see where you're coming from. When people uncover the root-cause problem, they want to get on and solve the problem but (and far be it from me to hold people back) let me make a case for looking at what the diagram is telling you. It's giving you everything you ever needed to know about the problem in all its manifestations. It's the perfect blend of IQ and EQ, keeping the problems separate, which stops people feeling they've been swallowed up but also showing how the problems connect and their root-cause. And it provides an excellent way of briefing people who weren't part of the problem-solving process because it doesn't just show the end result, it shows the thinking process and that means people can see, and relate to, it's common sense.

Then expose the core-conflict

Your last task in this part of the problem-solving process is to look closely at the root-cause problem itself. Because within that will be a core-conflict. And that's the other reason I wanted you to pause and reflect on the cause-and-effect diagram. It was to shore up your resilience for when you have to face up to the core-conflict. You might feel a little deflated when you see how un-resolvable it looks but take heart – you've finally reached the point where you're ready to make the problem disappear!

IN SHORT

▶ **Isolate the problems before you connect them.** What's your experience of the challenge of trying to solve a problem at its root-cause?

▶ **Get a balance between logic and intuition.** Do you lean more towards left-brain, logical problem-solving techniques or right-brain, intuitive ones?

▶ **Make people's emotions part of the process.** Do you wish you could run from the emotional aspects of a problem?

14

How do you shift people's thinking to make the problem disappear?

Surfacing hindering beliefs and getting rid of the core-conflict

Conflict – good, bad or just inevitable?

Conflict gives us information about what's important and alerts us to the need to take action. If you choose to see it as helpful, it can become the catalyst in a challenging situation that leads to transformational progress. The main problem with conflict is that we aren't comfortable with it, especially in organizations. Yet, I've always found that when I stop getting upset and start engaging with what the opposing voices are saying I end up with a far better solution than I'd have got if everyone had agreed in the first place.

From judging to analyzing

This chapter offers a way of making the core-conflict in any problem disappear but it requires a frame of mind that sees conflict as an opportunity. It also requires people to analyze their needs and beliefs to give them not only the information they need to make the problem disappear, but to get them out of judging mode because it's the judgements we make about conflict that make it negative. And have I mentioned it's always easier to get someone to stop doing something by getting them to start doing something else?

Dig down – because there are more needs than the ones in the core-conflict

Have you noticed when you're in conflict with someone how your whole relationship ends up being reduced to the one need that isn't being met? It's true – a conflict focuses the mind on what's going wrong but needs that *are* being met can get overlooked in the process. And when we don't take the whole picture into account, we can find ourselves trying to satisfy our unmet need in ways that undermine our other needs. And don't tell me you've never won an argument to the detriment of a relationship. In the problem from Part 1, people had more needs than just to protect themselves. They needed to be respected for their expertise, producing successful projects, enjoying their job and so on.

Then rise above – to find your common purpose

Now, put the conflict on one side for a while and focus on why your working relationship with the other person exists so you can establish your common purpose and raise your level of thinking beyond the problem. The common purpose of all the parties in the project management problem was to bring in projects on time, within budget, to specification and to customer satisfaction.

Do a health check on your common purpose

Sadly, it's all too common for two parties to be bound together in a common purpose that's as healthy as someone supplying drink to an alcoholic partner. A healthy common purpose creates a positive experience and, an unhealthy one creates a negative experience. And if you're worried that you can't know which it is until you've tried it, try thinking through the consequences. Look at your common purpose and work out all the consequences of achieving it. You'll know you've done it properly if your list includes positives and negatives (because nothing is totally one or the other) and you'll know it's healthy if the positives greatly outweigh the negatives. A more right-brained way to check is just to slow down and give your intuition a chance to make you more aware. Then, if you get a 'that's okay' feeling, go with it, but if you get an 'off' feeling go back and rethink things.

Beneath needs and common purpose lie beliefs

To get at beliefs, you need to look at the needs and common purpose you've identified and ask what someone would have to believe (about themselves, other people, the world at large) to make the connections. Once you've surfaced the beliefs, you can challenge them to see if they're helping or hindering the achievement of the common purpose. With the project-management problem, the belief that being self-serving would protect people didn't help the common purpose at all. That there's a problem to be solved suggests you'll find at least some hindering beliefs so if at first you don't succeed, keep looking.

Nature abhors a vacuum – especially human nature

When you challenge a hindering belief you leave a vacuum – so you need to replace it with a helpful belief. In the project-management problem, the belief that the best way to avoid pain was to 'look after number one' was replaced by the belief that the best way to avoid pain is to be 'one-for-all-and-all-for-one'. And the same applies to any problem you make disappear, as we'll explore in the next chapter.

IN SHORT

▶ **Conflict is an opportunity for transformational change.** What's your instinctive reaction to that statement and what do you think your reaction says about you?

▶ **Focus on all the needs, not just the unmet ones.** Have you ever won the battle only to lose the war?

▶ **Challenge the beliefs that are driving the behaviour.** How deep do you dig when you're dealing with a problem?

15

How do you fill the space left by the problem with something better?

Problems exist to raise our thinking to a new level of possibility

The gift a problem brings

It can be tempting, once you've made the problem disappear, to turn to other things, but it would be a shame to overlook the gift the problem has left behind – the stakeholders' commitment to the common purpose. When our subconscious creates negative experiences (problems) to get us to challenge our hindering beliefs, it doesn't just want us to get rid of them, it wants us to replace them with helping beliefs and create positive experiences.

Creating a vision that expresses the common purpose

According to research, some people are drawn towards seeking pleasure and others towards avoiding pain. I do know that some people seem to find it naturally easier to develop a vision of a pleasurable future state than others, whose vision for tomorrow is just the absence of today's problems. Either way, having a cause-and-effect diagram helps – the people whose vision tends to be of problem-free zone can produce a compelling vision from finding the opposite of the problem statements. And the rest can use the diagram as a springboard to a creative brainstorm.

Painting in the details that make the picture come alive

Forget everything you've read about visions needing to be sound-bite-size statements (which mean different things to different people) and think of building a mental picture that's real to people – with detail, nuances, light and shade. Think about how people will be behaving towards each other in the desired future state, their attitudes as well as their tasks. Imagine the future has happened and you're living it. And don't tell me it's too airy-fairy because we do it every time we get so caught up in a film that we feel transported to a different place, culture or age.

Notice anything that feels 'off'

One way of doing this is to do a 'walkthrough' of a day in the life of each stakeholder in the desired future state. As each person describes their day, the rest of the group can be alert to anything that doesn't feel right and help adjust the vision. There are people who'd quite happily rehearse a presentation who think rehearsing a new way of behaving sounds daft but it works, and in the real world, that's what counts. A 'walkthrough' isn't just a good way of picking up the small details of the vision, it's also a way of tricking the subconscious,

CREATING SOMETHING BETTER

which can't differentiate between actual experience and imagined experience (which is why visualization techniques work) into helping achieve it, as we'll see in the next chapter.

Prepare for the action plan stage by making a list

Real change involves change at belief level but, as we can't know what's in people's heads, we get to beliefs through behaviour. If, as you do the 'walkthrough', you make notes of the kinds of things people are saying, it can become an action list. Some of the things that often appear on my lists are:

- Keeping each other informed, communicating better and more often.
- Involving people in decisions and at an earlier stage.
- More thinking before acting, more manual, less autopilot.
- Asking more questions and challenging more assumptions, taking less for granted.
- Giving each other feedback and a reliable basis from which to adjust course.

Finding the beliefs that underpin the new behaviours

As you can see, there are behaviours that need to happen on a day-to-day basis (which is why I hammer on about sweating the small stuff) but when change takes place at belief level, behaviour change flows effortlessly from the new belief. So take each item on the list and ask what someone must believe to behave like that. Ask what beliefs would enable their subconscious to

When change takes place at belief level, behaviour change flows effortlessly.

automatically pull them towards, say, communicating more often? Perhaps they need to believe good communication is an important end in its own right or maybe they believe it's a useful step in the process towards getting a better output. And to find out what has to change to allow the new belief to take root, you need to think about what beliefs the same people must have that prevent them communicating well now. Remember that we can't hold two opposing thoughts (which is all a belief is) at the same time because our brains can't cope with cognitive dissonance.

Cognitive dissonance happens when we try to hold two opposing thoughts at the same time. The mind can't cope with it, so works hard to get rid of the inconsistency [dissonance] in one of three ways:

1. By reducing the importance of the dissonant beliefs.

2. By increasing the number of consistent beliefs to outweigh the dissonant ones.

3. By reinterpreting the dissonant beliefs so they're no longer inconsistent.

I know a smoker who uses all three!

The existing belief must be challenged, dropped to make room for the new one, which also helps when lapses occur (as they do when we're stressed) as the new belief can be sustained through brief periods of cognitive dissonance caused by old beliefs resurfacing.

Remember, every stakeholder is different

Let me assure you we're not talking about a cloning exercise where every stakeholder has to buy into the same set of beliefs before signing up to a shared vision. As the communication example shows, you can share a vision but have different beliefs. It's not about uniformity, it's about compatibility – on two levels:

- *Compatible with the vision* – so beliefs sustain the stakeholder through the change.
- *Compatible with the rest of their belief system* – so they don't end up with conflicting intentions, leaving their subconscious to sabotage their efforts.

Listen carefully to what people are saying. Do they sound like they're struggling to convince themselves? Are they saying all the right words but somehow not convincing you?

When we're observing and listening, our conscious picks up the words and the more obvious behaviour and our subconscious picks up the rest. Because **our subconscious notices everything** and because it's stronger than our conscious, we tend to form our judgements from the way people behave rather than what they say. Our **subconscious is designed to spot inconsistencies**, which it tells us about through our intuition. Because all this happens below our level of consciousness, we often just get a feeling that we don't trust someone, but if we analyzed it we'd find we've picked up an inconsistency between their words and deeds.

If so, chances are they're operating on a conscious level only and won't be able to sustain the change because their subconscious mind is in conflict. Keep working with them to find beliefs that work for them. And take heart – it may seem like a struggle at times but it's worth the wait to see someone's eyes light up when they suddenly see a new logic.

IN SHORT

▶ **Don't just solve the problem, put something better in its place.** Do you ever just let the buzz you get from solving a problem go flat?

▶ **Create a vision for a better future.** What do your visions say about you – are you someone who moves towards pleasure or away from pain?

▶ **Find the beliefs that fit the vision.** Have you ever experienced self-sabotage that came from clashing beliefs?

16

How do you turn the vision into reality?

Making self-sustaining decisions and adjust-as-you-go-action plans

What is a self-sustaining decision anyway?

We're all familiar with decisions that involve massive effort to keep them in place when all around us (including ourselves if we're honest) just want to slip quietly back into the old ways. Well, self-sustaining decisions do exactly what they say on the tin – they sustain themselves so you don't have to do anything. When we make decisions using only our conscious minds we're in 'push' mode – which means we're constantly monitoring ourselves to be sure our behaviour is supporting the decision (and that's hard work). But when we get our subconscious mind on board, we're in 'pull' mode. And that means our subconscious is gently pulling us towards acting out the behaviour that supports our decision. And because we're not conscious of our subconscious (that went without saying,

> **Self-sustaining decisions do exactly what they say on the tin.**

didn't it?) it doesn't feel like an effort to sustain our decision. It happens naturally.

Developing complete and congruent action plans

We all have our favourite approach for developing an action plan and I wouldn't dream of asking you to adopt mine. Just consider incorporating the following two points in yours to make sure your action plans get both maximum 'push' *and* 'pull' benefits:

- *Ensure the plan is complete* – including any tasks needed to bed in the desired new behaviours, the kind ordinary action plans tend to leave out as they aren't directly part of delivering the task. So, if you want people to keep each other informed more often, you might want to include an item in your action plan on regular meetings.

- *Ensure the plan is congruent* – by checking that all the tasks in the action plan are compatible with the beliefs that underpin the behaviour changes you are seeking. Too many attempts to empower people have failed because the empowerment strategy used top-down briefing methods that clash with the concept of an empowered culture.

With built-in flexibility to adjust-as-you-go

Sticklers plan down to the last detail, their plans are works of art in their own right, which is maybe why they stick to them whether they're working or not. Go-with-the-flow types don't plan, they want lots of room for manoeuvre but their lack of a plan for getting feedback

Structure the plan in broad terms only, but create a management process.

often means they get their manoeuvring wrong. The both/and solution is to structure the plan in broad terms only, but create a management process that gives you all the input you need to fill in the detail later and to adjust-as-you-go.

When people **administer** a process they are in essence just processing their bits of it. And **co-ordinating** is just about ensuring other people process their bits. **Managing** is what people are doing when they are making sure that what is supposed to be happening *is* happening, and doing something about it, if it's not.

Creating a management process

Talking of management, people often confuse it with administering or co-ordinating.

To manage, you need to have a radar system that gives you the information you need to answer two questions:

- What do you have to put in place so that you know that what is supposed to be happening is actually happening?
- How will you know that what is being produced is of the right quality?

Once you know what information you need, you can put in place mechanisms to gather that information from the people who are implementing parts of the action plan.

And setting up a report-back mechanism

You won't be the only person implementing the action plan so, as you can't be everywhere at once, you need other people watching the radar screen too, letting you know the instant they pick up anything unusual. And that's all a report-back is, a short email/phone call to you (or to all the problem-solving group members if you prefer) at the time the variation occurs (timing is critical). Report-backs give you the chance to make an *immediate* tactical adjustment. Variations can be a real blessing in disguise because they make us stop and think (whether we have time to do it or not) and:

- Establish the root-cause of the variation.

- Challenge our existing expectations of what should be happening to see if they need to change.

- Identify options for action to get back on track with the original action plan or to modify the action plan (and, with that, our expectations of what should be happening).

- Decide which is our best option and implement it.

- Go back to watching the radar screen.

And bringing the problem-solving group together for reviews for learning

If report-backs happen as and when variations appear on the radar screen, reviews for learning can take place at more planned intervals. Giving people the chance to share their experience with the rest of the group allows everyone to learn from the experience of all group members, not just from their own. The group then talks through what, if anything, their insight is telling them and makes strategic adjustments.

Providing emotional support for behaviour change

Changing beliefs is a deeply personal change so, in addition to planning and managing implementation, you may need to provide emotional support during the transition period.

> I want to distinguish **emotions** from **feelings**. Emotions are mental states [coming from our thoughts] and feelings are physical sensations. Emotions can generate feelings, as with anger and a tight feeling in the chest, but they are separate. The same feeling can be associated with two emotions – for example, a churning stomach can be fear or excitement depending on our thoughts about the situation we're in.

If emotion is thought, it follows that changing the thoughts someone is having will change their emotions. So, when people are discouraged or demotivated, try the following:

■ *Suspend judgement and start from where they are* – it doesn't matter whether they're right, wrong, exaggerating or distorting, because if they believe they've got a problem, they've got a problem. Take their emotions as fact and help them solve the problem that's causing them to think that way. Once they're focused on solving the problem, they'll feel more positive.

■ *Don't invalidate their emotions* – have you noticed the kind of things people say to encourage you when you're discouraged – things like, 'You can do it' or 'It's not that bad'? And have you thought about what they're actually saying? They're saying, 'You're wrong'!

- *Watch out for hindering beliefs* – and help people challenge them. It's impossible to identify every hindering belief in the earlier stages of the problem-solving process because they often only come to the fore when they're challenged so be prepared to help people deal with them.

- *Don't give praise or criticism, give neutral feedback* – a matter-of-fact, but highly observant account of the detail of their performance tells them you've really *seen* what they've done and will help them become more self-reliant and deal with negative feedback which in turn will give them more faith in their own judgement.

- *Believe in them when they don't believe in themselves* – when people are struggling, the first thing that suffers is their self-confidence. Look for what you know to be fundamentally true about them and make that the foundation of your belief in them.

- *If in doubt, ask what they need from you* – we all have different needs for emotional support at different times and the only way we can be sure we're getting it right is to ask the people we're supporting about their best and worst experiences of being emotionally supported.

IN SHORT

▶ **Plans must be complete and congruent.** Do your plans always include actions in support of belief and attitude changes?

▶ **Don't just *do* the task, *manage* it.** Do you always have a process for managing the task as well as for doing it?

▶ **Get the best radar system you can.** How do you know if what's supposed to be happening is actually happening?

▶ **Provide appropriate emotional support.** Do you create strong, empowered people or helpless dependants?

PART

3

■ *real* management for the way it is ■

Knowing when thinking needs to shift

▶ **Getting unstuck**

No matter how good the problem-solving process you've developed is, there will be times when people get stuck. That's when they need you to facilitate the process. Have you ever listened to yourself think? It's simply the process of asking ourselves questions and answering them and the quality of our thinking comes from the quality of the questions we ask ourselves.

This part of the book explores the different kinds of occasions when people tend to get stuck – usually when they're in an inappropriate thinking mode for that stage of the problem-solving process. It explains how to recognize those occasions and how to shift the way people are thinking so they can give the problem the right kind of focus.

▶ Don't just take my word for it – check it against your own experience

As you read this part think back to your last experience of problem solving and review it against what you're reading.

17

When does the answer seem immediately obvious?

The need to shift from autopilot to manual thinking

Our brains are designed for autopilot problem solving

These days for most of us, most of the time, our survival doesn't depend on the speed of our thinking (okay, it may feel like that sometimes when the boss is breathing down our necks), it depends on the quality. So we really don't need a brain that looks quickly for similarities with a problem it's already solved and recycles the same old response. Neither do we need our RAS to stop us noticing anything that makes us question our choice of autopilot solution. Incidentally, this is why learning to listen and look for what feels 'off' is the single biggest perceiving and thinking skill any manager can acquire. It's the only sure-fire way of you being in manual control of both your RAS and your pre-programmed responses.

Learning to listen and look for what feels 'off' is the single biggest perceiving and thinking skill any manager can acquire.

There's nothing wrong with autopilot thinking

I hope you know me well enough by now (have you read the appendix yet?) to know that I don't think anything is inherently bad (or good for that matter), so of course I'm not saying that manual thinking is always good and autopilot thinking is always bad. I'm saying, like I do for characteristics, events, emotions and so on, that autopilot thinking is neutral – meaning that it's sometimes helpful and sometimes hindering depending on the context. It's helpful when:

- We're responding to emergencies and operating on an instinct which somehow enables us to know the right thing to do without knowing how we know.

- We're 'in the zone' doing what we do best (now why do I always get a mental picture of David Beckham taking a free kick on the edge of the box whenever I think of unconscious competence?)

Or with immediate answers – when they're Eureka moments

You might also be forgiven for thinking I'm sceptical about the value of the instant solution, but I'm not. The very act of being fully engaged with your work, totally absorbed in what you're doing, can make the solution seem obvious simply because it is obvious – no mental trickery involved. Have you ever had a Eureka moment? Doesn't it always come after a long period of what might seem like fruitless engagement with a problem?

So how do you know when you're getting into autopilot trouble?

Ask yourself (or the person you suspect of autopilot thinking) what other options they considered and rejected. If there aren't any, they're on autopilot. Timing is a big clue too, so watch out for them coming up with answers before getting engaged with the issues.

Understanding our natural response cycle so we can use it to our advantage

Something happens to stimulate a response, we process the stimulus (whatever we've seen, heard and so on) against what's stored in our subconscious then, when we find a similar stimulus and a pre-programme that tells us how we responded last time, we select that and use it to respond. Then we get feedback (which becomes stimulus) and we do the whole process again, adjusting as we go. Sometimes our autopilot response is the best response but if we just launch into it without checking, we won't know that until it's too late. Admit it – how many times have you reacted instantly to something (when emotions were running high) only to regret it afterwards? And how many times have you held back and done the logical thing – and regretted that too? Well . . . you do know that whoever said life was easy was only having us on. I didn't ask those questions to have a go at you, if only because I'd be in a glass house throwing stones. I just think we need to develop our own pre-programme complete with an autopilot response that gives us the best chance of getting the right response.

The react-now-respond-later pre-programme

This is a less cruel variation of the go-home-and-kick-the-cat pre-programme. It works with our natural response cycle so we don't lose the benefits of having our subconscious on board but it also brings our conscious mind into play so we give ourselves choices. It starts when something happens and we process it and then we react. But – and this is the big difference – we react in our mind, we don't act it out in real life. We let our autopilot response surface from our subconscious into our conscious mind and have a look at it before putting it into action. We don't block it in case it *is* the best solution but we don't act on it yet in case it's not. So much for 'react now', next is 'respond later'.

Counting to ten, sleeping on it – finding what works for you

You know the old 'count to ten' thing – it didn't become a cliché for nothing. Most emotional reactions don't last long so that by the time you've counted to ten (or ten thousand if, like me, you're a sensitive soul) your reaction has changed and, if you responded while in the height of your emotional state you're probably regretting it. The time it takes to come down from an emotional high varies from person to person, from stimulus to stimulus and from context to context but if we look back at our experience we can usually work out how long it takes us to get back to a state of relative equilibrium. I know that most work upsets only need me to sleep on them to get my perspective back but a bad experience with someone important to me takes much, much longer. So, I delay my response until I've processed my reaction and avoid making matters worse. Okay, not always but I never claimed to be perfect!

Using the pause to bring our conscious mind on board

We've surfaced our subconscious, instinctive reaction but we've not acted it out and then we've paused to let our emotions settle a bit. Now we bring in our conscious and all of its logic. We do that by (you guessed it) asking ourselves questions. I know you're busy so I'll give you the questions I use and you can adapt them to suit you. Why not pick a situation where you reacted but wished you'd responded and go over it again, asking these questions:

1. *What was the stimulus for my reaction and is there any other way of interpreting that stimulus?* No matter how quickly you react, you've still processed the stimulus – that is, interpreted an event to make an experience of it. An example. I hate it when I'm in full flow of enthusiasm for a project and someone brings me crashing back to earth with a 'yes but' and all sorts of sensible worries. My instinctive reaction involves acts of verbal violence . . . what can I say, I don't like being tethered. But I know I could also interpret it as an attempt to keep me grounded which I need.

2. *What do I want to achieve with my response and will my autopilot reaction get me that?* This is where you tap into your logical mind's ability to see the bigger picture. In my example, I can tell you what going with my reaction achieves (because I've done it often enough I'm ashamed to say). It stops the other person being negative but ultimately, it creates a negative experience for me because it gives me what I want at the expense of what I need plus it damages my relationship.

3. *What other options for responding do I have?* Well, there's always the put-up-with-it-because-it's-good-for-me response but that doesn't work because my feelings are hurt by the negativity and it doesn't accommodate that or my self-protective need to say no to any attempt to stop me when I'm in full creative flow.

4. *Which option gets me everything I need and makes common sense (appealing both to the logic of my conscious mind and the intuition of my subconscious mind)?* Well, what do I want? I want to be able to go with the full flow of my creativity and then think of the practical constraints afterwards. I want to get across how it makes me feel to be greeted with negativity but I also want to be kept grounded. And I want to suggest we work out a way of getting the best of both worlds.

So, there you have it. Go through the process and stick with your intuitive autopilot response if you still think it's best on reflection. Or throw it away and go with your logic. Or find a both/and response. It's your choice and your responsibility.

I like the definition of **responsibility** that describes it as **response-ability**. Being responsible means that in our moments of choice, we recognize that we don't just have to react, we can respond. It means looking at our options for responding, weighing up the potential consequences of each option, deciding which one will achieve the best results, and responding on that basis.

And it's as simple as not forcing yourself to ignore your natural reaction but making that reaction a step in a bigger, more considered response process. You'll notice I've used the generic words 'stimulus' and 'response' in the questions above. I did that because I wanted you to see that this method is useful for all kinds of situations. But if you want to tailor the questions for use with a problem-solving group – just substitute problem for stimulus and solution for response and the same questions apply.

And don't forget to watch out for your RAS because perception is all

When you feel that you or a group you're working with is in danger of leaping to immediate solutions on autopilot, try thinking about the way you/they are seeing the problem and ask:

- Does this problem remind anyone of other problems we've solved in the past? What are the similarities between this problem and those problems? And what are the differences (because there are bound to be some)? Stick with those differences because they're what will get people off autopilot.

And when a solution is presented with worrying haste ask:

- Is that the obvious solution? Does it involve a pattern of behaviour that we've used a lot in the past in response to similar problems? What other solutions have we considered and rejected and why?

Once you've got yourself or others out of autopilot and onto manual, then you can go back to the standard problem-solving process described in Part 2.

IN SHORT

▶ **Understand how your brain works so you control it instead of it controlling you.** How often do you operate on autopilot?

▶ **Develop a response programme that works for you.** How would your team describe you – as a reactor or a responder?

▶ **Get your conscious and subconscious aligned.** Are your responses more often instinctive, logical or a bit of both?

18

When does the solution just create another problem?

The need to shift from symptomatic to root-cause thinking

What is symptomatic thinking?

Symptomatic thinking happens when people start working on solutions to the problem without first thinking about what's causing the problem. The trouble is, we don't always spot symptomatic thinking at the time it's happening. But we notice it later on when we're dealing with the consequences, which are yet more problems.

The popularity of the 'quick and dirty' approach

I once had a boss who favoured the 'quick and dirty' approach to achieving organizational change. He didn't rate his senior management colleagues' ability to innovate and his solution was the classic 'we need new blood'. He encouraged a few senior managers to retire early and filled their posts with external recruits with good track records of innovating. Simple and effective, right? Wrong. Many of the people he recruited either learned to conform to the prevailing risk-averse culture or left because they felt stifled by it. What's more, he managed to create another problem – namely, demotivated internal staff, who watched their promotion opportunities disappear and who resented outsiders getting the plum jobs. Which meant that any external recruits who didn't surrender to the cultural norms had trouble getting support for their innovations.

That solves the wrong problem

Have you, like me, spent your career under constant pressure to come up with quick-fix solutions and one-minute answers? It can push most of us into treating the symptom rather than the cause at times and for some it becomes the standard method of operating. Well, let's face it, we all know the response we're likely to get if we ask for more time – it doesn't just happen to football managers!

Seeing the signs – negative side-effects, hindering beliefs and no connections

Negative side-effects are one way of spotting symptomatic solutions. And you don't have to wait until they appear; you can anticipate them by asking people to think specifically about the likely side-effects of a particular solution. The next sign is hindering beliefs. In the example of the preference my boss had for the 'quick and dirty' approach, he believed that our long-serving, home-grown managers couldn't be developed to be innovative. That's a sweeping generalization, a prejudice even, and a prime example of a hindering belief. So, when you hear a solution, ask yourself what the person must believe to think that's the answer and see if you can spot any hindering beliefs. Finally, it's a classic sign of symptomatic thinking when people can't see any connections between their problem and other problems. All problems have links to other problems and failure to find them accounts for most of the energy that we waste at work when we try to solve problems.

I'm not saying symptomatic solutions are a bad thing

Let's be realistic. The need for symptomatic solutions will never go away so, of course, they deserve a place in the *real* manager's toolkit. In my example, there was nothing wrong with filling some posts externally, provided its side-effects were managed and work was done in parallel to discover what was causing senior managers to be risk-averse and lacking in innovation in the first place. I feel like I'm stating the blindingly obvious here but if it were blindingly obvious then we'd all be doing it already . . . and we aren't.

People can only do what they can do

The last time I gave in to an urge to get fit (I usually sit down with a cup of tea and wait for it to pass) I bought an exercise tape. As I watched it (well, you didn't expect me to do it, did you?) I heard the instructor talk about her eighty-year old mother who was doing the exercises slightly differently to the younger participants. She said, 'She's only doing what she can do'. There was something about that expression that seemed to apply to life in general and it's stuck with me ever since. It certainly summed up the situation with two friends of mine. They were professional chefs and the wife was facing a serious medical problem. Throughout her ordeal, the husband cooked her fabulous meals, coming home after putting in long hours in the kitchen at work to put in long hours in their kitchen. He couldn't give her emotional support (he was even more scared than she was) so he did what he could do and cooked for her instead. Why do we cook for people who need emotional support? Because it's not as if we can honestly say we think it's going to solve the problem. It's something to do with our fear of being incapable of dealing with the real issue but not wanting to feel helpless, so we do the thing we *can* do.

And that's a shame because the sneaky thing about root-causes is that they are never as hard to resolve as people fear. On the contrary, they're often much easier to solve than some of the symptomatic problems and they don't bring negative side-effects – though, luckily for my chef friend, his wife understood and appreciated what he was doing, because if she hadn't, it would have only made things worse. Talk of fears always brings me to talk of beliefs, because behind every fear is a belief that needs to be challenged. In the example of my 'quick and dirty' boss, he didn't even question his belief that internal managers weren't innovative. And his RAS (intent on proving him right) made sure he didn't notice the strong counter-evidence that our organization was well managed by the very people he didn't rate.

Root-causes are never as hard to resolve as people fear.

Shifting to root-cause thinking

The IQ solution for shifting from symptomatic thinking to root-cause thinking is simple – just keep asking, 'Why does that problem happen?' until you run out of causes. But, bear in mind that, as we've seen, symptomatic thinking isn't always an IQ problem. It can be an EQ problem and you might need to recognize people's fears and work with them, surfacing hindering beliefs and gently challenging them. So, if someone says the unions won't accept radical change – look into their fears and find a way of addressing them, for example by ensuring they are involved as a key stakeholder.

IN SHORT

▶ **Don't use symptomatic solutions unless you're prepared for the side-effects.** Have you ever solved a problem only to find your solution only created another problem?

▶ **Watch out for hindering beliefs.** Are your rationales for your proposed solutions ever based on hindering beliefs?

▶ **Work with the fear but don't let it rule.** Have you ever been scared of the repercussions of digging too deep?

19

When does it seem like there's no solution?

The need to shift from in-the-problem to above-the-problem thinking

The downside of engaging with the problem

So far, we've dealt with what happens when people don't engage with the problem but what happens when they get so absorbed in the problem they can't see anything else? The upside is they're building a solid foundation from which to have a Eureka moment. The downside is they can end up not being able to see beyond, above and around it. And that can leave them feeling very stuck.

'Get out of the box' as Einstein's spin doctor might have said

If I remember correctly, Einstein said, 'You can't solve problems at the same level of thinking that created them'. But if he'd lived today who knows what sound-bites 'sources close to Einstein' might have given us. What I take from his assertion is that the idea is to get your mind above the problem so you can look it from outside the box it's in.

So many ways of getting above-the-problem

There are lots of books full of creative-thinking techniques. I've tried and had fun with many – especially the idea of opening the dictionary and picking a word at random then thinking about the problem in the context of that word. Or making a list of different occupations and thinking about how they'd look at the problem – lawyer, clergyman, policeman etc. In the rest of this chapter I'd like to focus on my three favourites.

One word, one definition, many meanings

This is a good after-dinner game (I can only tell you this because you already know how sad I am). I call it the 'denotations/connotations' game – denotation being the dictionary definition and connotation being the meaning we give to the word – but then I loved English Grammar at school (see what I mean about sad). It's a simple game. Someone makes a statement and the rest of us guess what else it tells us. So, I might say, for example, 'There were lots of Portuguese restaurants in Stockwell in the early 1990s' and the others see what they can surmise from that statement, about me, about Stockwell and so on. I'd give you the answers so you can see if you're right, but I don't want you to become as sad as I am, now do I?

At work, the game is imminently more practical and based listening out for examples of people appearing to use words that don't make sense in the context of the rest of what they're saying. For example, I was working with a manager who was complaining about his staff. He cited examples of where they just do their bit and pass it on to the next person in the chain, so that there was no continuity and no one taking responsibility for seeing the task through. He said he wished they were more flexible. That word didn't fit the rest of what he was saying so I knew he was giving it a connotation that didn't match its denotation. I guessed that with his ex-trade union representative hat on he saw the whole problem as some kind of demarcation issue (people doing what's in their job description and only that), hence his use of the word 'flexibility'. I tested understanding which saved me from training his staff in the wrong skill.

Now, how does this help us get from in-the-problem to above-the-problem? Well, we need to challenge the connotations of the words we use to define a problem. Let's take a problem a publisher had in selling 50,000 copies of a management book whose proceeds were going to charity. Now think about what connotations people put onto the words 'management book'. Something a manager buys to read? That connotation takes you down the road of a problem about attracting 50,000 managers to buy one copy each. But, playing

We need to challenge the connotations of the words we use to define a problem.

the connotations game, you'd ask when is a book not a book? And the answer is when it's a corporate gift, a conference pack freebie or a learning resource. And suddenly you've shifted from in-the-problem to above-the-problem thinking with the realization that if persuading companies to buy the books as gifts for employees, conference organizers to include it in conference packs and local authorities to buy it for their libraries, reduces the number of people who need to buy it by increasing the number of copies each buys.

Finding a similar problem you've solved in the past

I can almost hear you saying, 'But didn't she tell me not to do that a few chapters ago'? And you'd be right. She did. But this is about exploiting our natural autopilot reaction not being exploited by it. For instance, I'd never run a training course for 200 people at a time but I had to run a conference for 200 people and in terms of event management there are many similarities between training and conferences so I used my experience of that problem to help with my current problem. I didn't replicate my earlier experience, because there were significant differences, I just used it to get me out of the box I'd put the problem into. And it doesn't have to be a previous work problem – it can be anything that's analogous to the problem situation. So, for example, with a poor performer you might think about what a football manager might do with a problem player if transfer isn't an option. He could loan him out to another team which would stop him dragging his own team down and might even improve his performance. Do you see what I mean?

And finally – looking for the dependencies

The final method of getting from in-the-problem to above-the-problem is to look for any apparent dependencies that aren't really there. I had a problem getting managers to complete appraisal forms on time and to a decent quality. The self-imposed dependency in the problem was that it was the manager who had to complete the forms. I say self-imposed because they don't have to. The manager has to hold the appraisal discussion and agree what's on the form but each appraisee can write up their own form.

Find your own techniques

These are my favourites but what counts is what works for you. Try them and, if you like them, keep them but ask around and see what other people do. Start a collection of your own.

IN SHORT

▶ **Beware the downside of engaging with the problem.** Do you ever find that when you get really absorbed in a problem, you can't see beyond it?

▶ **Collect a range of techniques for your problem-solving toolkit.** What different kinds of problem-solving techniques do you use?

20

When do people feel powerless to solve the problem?

The need to shift from constraint to possibility thinking

People make the box smaller than it is

Someone I know once observed that if people at work have X amount of room to manoeuvre most of them will play safe by doing their job within 'X minus Y margin for safety'. It was something I hadn't noticed for myself (perhaps because I've always had a tendency to give myself 'X plus Z amount I think I can get away with') but, as with anything that stimulates our RAS, I began to notice it all the time after that.

Powerless versus powerful – it's all a matter of belief

How powerful are you? If you rated your power at work, what would you factor into your calculations? People talk about their authority and subtract the power of other people to constrain them – including their boss, their customers, unions and so on. What I've particularly noticed is the tendency people have to underestimate their own power and overestimate other people's. Which is understandable when you think about it. What's the first thing we learn when we start work – okay, apart from where the toilets are? The rules about what we can and can't do. You don't have to be Max Weber to know that bureaucracies and their hierarchical authority structures survive on the fact that we all conform to their cultural norms. Just ask yourself, how many times have you bowed to the authority of someone you wouldn't give the time of day to if they weren't higher up the ladder than you? In colluding with the rules of hierarchy, we all become conditioned to giving our power away to our so-called 'superiors'. I'm not saying this is a bad thing per se (I have nothing against power used for the greater good) and without it some would argue we'd have anarchy, all I'm saying is that it often leaves people thinking they can do less than they actually can. It boils down to this. We are as powerful or powerless as we believe we are. So, the facilitator of a problem-solving group needs to be on the lookout for signs that the group (or individuals within it) is making its box smaller than it is. But what signs?

People think they can do less than they actually can.

Listening out for constraint thinking

Have you noticed how people can be so busy talking they don't actually hear what they're saying? Like the team member I had who swore he thrived on change but who started every other sentence with the words 'yes, but'. I once, only to be mischievous I swear, kept a little tally (just the five-bar gate kind) of how many times he used 'yes, but' in a team meeting and showed him the results afterwards. He genuinely didn't hear himself say it so he had no idea he was coming across negatively. Sometimes, when people are telling you the 3,000 reasons why they can't solve that problem, they'll think they're just explaining the realities of life and won't realize that they're actually saying they feel powerless. So, when you hear the 'yes, but' arguments coming out, you know people have gone into constraint thinking. Now it's useful to be able to identify and understand the constraints but we all know the difference between someone talking about constraints in a 'and this is how we'll manage it' way and someone who is talking about them in a 'which means we can't do it, I'm afraid' way. It's the latter who need their thinking shifted.

The aikido approach

The natural temptation, when someone starts talking negatively, is to try to win them over by countering their point. But have you noticed how that only succeeds in making them cling even more tightly to their position? The best thing is to work with their negative energy by asking ask them to list all the way in which the constraint hinders progress. Go into detail, really engage with their issues. Then ask them to list the ways in which the constraint is helpful. This does two things:

- It gets them thinking instead of judging because by the time they tell you the constraint they've made their minds up so you need to get them to rethink. And, as everything is neutral, there *will* be a helpful aspect. I used to think having a boss who won't say yes without making you jump through hoops was a totally negative experience until I realized how much I was learning about influencing.

- Once they're thinking about the constraint as a neutral thing, they'll start to feel less constrained by it. And instead of being the obstacle that's preventing them from making progress, it will become just something else to be managed.

From constraints to possibilities

To get them to reposition the constraint as a point on a road to the solution they need to be able to see that there *is* road beyond the constraint . . . and that's where the big 'what if' question comes in. It speaks directly to their subconscious, giving it permission to believe the constraint has been removed (it plays on the fact that our subconscious can't distinguish fact from fiction). And what *is* the big 'what if' question? The one that says, 'Yes, Fred, I hear what you're saying but what if that constraint didn't exist, what would you do then?' All you're doing is artificially – openly and shamelessly – pretending the constraint has gone so people can move from constraint to possibility thinking. I guarantee you'll be pleasantly surprised at the possibilities their subconscious comes up with once you've released them from the prison their conscious mind has locked them in.

And self-empowerment to boot

Once they know what they want to achieve and they're thinking possibilities, the chances are high they'll find a way around the constraints. Because the constraint, quite simply, becomes less important when it's not the only thing you can see. Plus, in making the shift, they'll start to feel pulled towards what they want and that engages their subconscious in finding ways round the obstacle. The results can be spectacular. I've even experienced – and I almost hesitate to tell you this in case you get over-excited – people finding ways of making the constraint work *for* them so they don't have to manage around it at all. I had a boss who was well known for his meanness with requests for more resources but totally supportive of anything that made him look innovative. So, while my colleagues were being downsized, I managed to triple the size of both my staff and non-staff budgets over a four-year period simply by making sure any requests for extra resources showed all the innovations we'd achieve with them.

Using the power of the subconscious

I talked about power earlier because, in all this, you're trying to shift people from feeling powerless to powerful. But sometimes the feeling of powerlessness isn't just related to the particular problem, it's part of their self-image. Then you need to work at a deeper level. Do that by stepping out of the specific problem and asking each group member to tell the group about their best ever problem-solving experience. Ask about the obstacles they faced and how they overcame them. Then, as they tell you their story, watch the shift in them as their subconscious remembers the feelings associated with being an effective problem solver. And if they don't have an experience at work, take them to a different scenario – at home or in a leisure activity – because people who feel disempowered at work often have much more empowering experiences in the outside world.

What we focus on expands

It's natural that once we get into problem mode, we'll start seeing problems everywhere. The techniques in this chapter work *with* our hard-wiring by shifting our focus from problems to opportunities, which means that's what will expand instead.

IN SHORT

▸ **We all have more power than we think.** What's your most powerful problem-solving experience?

▸ **But a lot less authority.** Do you have experience of a general lack of respect for authority in your organization?

▸ **Ask the big 'what if' question.** How do you help people get around the obstacles and constraints they feel are in their way?

21

When is there no single solution that pleases everyone?

The need to shift from 'either/or' to 'both/and' thinking

'Win–win' is just another name for shabby compromise

This kind of stuck thinking is no different from any I've described, yet it scares people much more, perhaps because it's seen as a people issue rather than a stuck-thinking issue. And, of course, if you get unstuck by compromising it *does* become a people issue, because success largely depends on whether people are satisfied with the piece of the pie they got.

To be honest, I've never really understood the concept of 'win–win' when applied to a negotiated result that gives both parties some of what they want (it sounds more like 'lose–lose' to me). Maybe it's the kind of thinker I am – always focusing on the gaps – but I've heard too many stories of negotiations where A gives up to B something that B wants to get something A wants in return and vice versa. Now, I'm all in favour of a bit of give and take but let's not get carried away here. Most 'win–win' solutions are compromises in disguise and according to the dictionary that makes them a 'partial surrender of one's position'. Well, I'm not big on surrender – it sounds like settling for less than what's possible. I like 'both/and' solutions that answer the question 'what if we could find a way of getting everything you want and everything I want without having to compromise?'

Compromise is settling for less than what's possible.

Assuming there's an answer – arrogance versus confidence

The simple trick to achieving a 'both/and' solution is to assume there *is* one. I once had a team member who felt people unfairly called him arrogant. I gave him the benefit of the doubt as I hadn't observed any signs of arrogance but, as any self-respecting manager does, I was on the lookout for evidence that would help me decide one way or another. And, sure enough, we were tackling an apparently insoluble problem and I heard him say there was no answer that worked for everyone. I asked him how he knew and he said he'd been looking at it for days and if there was one, he'd have found it by now. I then asked him which of the following statements he thought was arrogant and which was confident:

- I can't think of the answer to this problem so there can't be one.

- I can't think of the answer to this problem but I'm sure if I keep working on it, I'll get there eventually.

Arrogance is dangerous in problem solving because it closes the mind. What do you think happens in your subconscious if it hears your conscious mind saying there's no solution? That's right. It ensures your belief that there is no solution is proved right.

Letting our creative subconscious find a 'both/and' solution

If, however, you assume there's an answer that's just out of your reach, you're saying to your subconscious, 'Why don't you have a look in the corners of my subconscious and see if you can find something to help me solve this problem?'. And your subconscious, which always wants you to be right, works like crazy to find you the solution. Sometimes, that's all it takes – the issuing of an instruction to your subconscious. But there is a technique you can use to help things along a little. Stop working on the problem and do something else. That's all. I remember working with a manager who was developing a communications strategy and I suggested he sit with a pad of paper at his side while he was watching TV at home that evening and just make notes of whatever came into his mind while he was watching. He was amazed by how much of what he watched triggered thoughts about communication. In making the suggestion, I had spoken directly to his subconscious mind, and it had watched the TV on a different level to the way his conscious mind had watched it, leaving him feeling as if each TV programme had been a master class in communications strategy.

Sceptical? Find an article in a magazine, read it as you would normally, see what thoughts pop into your head as you read and jot them down. Don't force anything, just notice your thoughts as they emerge. Now, read it again, but this time in character, any character as long as it's different from your own. Try being a conspiracy theorist or a master of political correctness (oh dear, I don't suppose if you *were* a 'master' of political correctness you'd want to claim that particular title) and see what thoughts emerge this time. Different huh? And all you did was tell your subconscious you were someone else.

From EQ mess to IQ smart thinking

I've always thought of myself as rubbish at interpersonal skills, added to which I'm incredibly pig-headed about compromising, so I have trouble managing conflicts of interest in the usual empathic, give and take style. That's why I use the method I'm describing here. And the really good thing about letting your subconscious find a 'both/and' solution is that it shifts the problem from being a scary EQ (emotional intelligence, people skills) type to being an IQ (task focused, brainteasing puzzle time) type. Which puts us back in our comfort zone.

IN SHORT

- **'Win–win' should never involve any 'lose–lose'.** Have you ever experienced solving a problem without anyone having to compromise?

- **Confidence supports problem solving, arrogance undermines it.** How would an unbiased observer describe your attitude to problems that you can't solve?

- **Tap into your creative subconscious.** Do you regularly find the answers to your problem in unexpected places – the bath, walking the dog and so on?

22

When is the solution taking too much effort to sustain?

The need to shift from 'push' to 'pull' thinking

Too much 'push', not enough 'pull'

You know you're in 'push' mode when it's hard work keeping things going. We've all experienced it – we can't seem to get past conscious competence mode into unconscious competence, so it never gets to the stage of feeling comfortable. We think longingly of the last time we made a change that seemed effortless. We were in 'pull' mode then which means that, instead of our weaker conscious mind pushing us forward, our stronger subconscious mind was pulling us along effortlessly. The trouble is, if our subconscious decides the change isn't in our best interests, it will not only ignore the directions our conscious (in 'push' mode) is giving us, it will sabotage our efforts. And it can do this because the subconscious is more powerful than the conscious.

Remember, it's 'both/and' not 'either/or'

I'm not saying that 'push' mode is bad or that you need to choose one method over the other. On the contrary, there's nothing wrong with giving the subconscious a conscious helping hand. I'm saying that when we're implementing a change (an unavoidable part of problem solving) we need to make sure we get our subconscious mind on board too. Because if we don't, come a time of stress (and all change brings stress) our subconscious mind will slip back into its comfortable old ways.

Finding a solution that works at belief level

Our subconscious works at a deep-rooted belief level so, to make the change stick at that level, we need to work out what beliefs supported the problem and what beliefs support the solution and replace the old beliefs with the new ones. The best way to do this is to look for the gains people got from behaving in accordance with the old beliefs and then find the negative experiences that came with that. If, for example, you want people to take responsibility, identify what they gained from being irresponsible so you can build equally powerful gains into the required behaviour. And you have to find the downside of their old beliefs by looking for the negative experiences those beliefs created. And there must be a negative experience, or there wouldn't be a problem, would there? Use that – make it worth their while to change their belief. Take the example of a manager who is constantly checking up on her staff. The payoffs for doing this are that it reduces the number and severity of mistakes. But the belief that underpins it, that her staff cannot be trusted, is essentially a hindering belief; the downside of which is that she's taking a lot of time away from their own hands-on work and she's created a negative atmosphere in the team.

And looking out for conflicting intentions

I remember a manager introducing a new service to customers for delivery by his front-line staff. He believed it would benefit customers and so did his staff. But it had only been in place for a few weeks when people started slipping back into the old ways. The manager complained it was just another example of them paying lip service to the customer and questioned their commitment. It turned out that the new process took three times longer than the old one and, because it happened often, it left the staff running to a stand still. So, while their conscious minds saw the logic of the change and were in favour of it, their subconscious minds saw extra work when they were already overworked and were sabotaging their efforts to stick to the new regime. I recommended the manager sit down with his front-line staff and say, look, we're agreed this is a good idea so let's see if we can find a way of implementing it so it doesn't increase your workload. And, between them, they managed to give the customers what they wanted *and* make life easier for themselves. And, you've guessed it, the change was sustained effortlessly.

Making changes at belief level

So, when people are saying they believe in the change but are struggling to sustain it, look at their underlying beliefs. Ask yourself, what would someone have to believe to want the desired future state. And then ask what must they have believed to sustain the problem state. Then think about what's different between the two sets of beliefs and make

changing those beliefs as much a part of your transition management plan as any other task on your action list.

IN SHORT

▶ **Pull is stronger than push.** Have you experienced the
difference between change that's effortless and change
that's hard work?

▶ **The best solutions bring change at belief level.** What's
your success rate in bringing about changes you only pay
lip service to?

■ *real* management for the way it is ■

Conclusion

▶ **Leaving the hard sell until last**

I think almost every book I've read on problem solving starts by selling you the benefits, presumably to motivate you to actually try their method. It seems more logical to me to assume that you're already motivated to want to try really solving problems at root-cause level, otherwise you wouldn't have bought the book.

▶ **Do you want the benefits enough to face up to the complexity?**

Not sure? Then read on . . .

23

Why should you persevere with *real* problem solving when it's so complex?

I can't answer that, I can only tell you why I persevere

Only you know why you bought this book and what it would take to motivate you to try some of the ideas I'm putting forward. All I can do is tell you what motivates me to solve problems at root-cause and what I get out of it.

It gives me a buzz to watch problems disappear like magic

Like most managers, I thrive on a sense of achievement and, for me, the tougher the problem, the greater the sense of achievement. There's a buzz to be had from solving a problem that people have hidden from for years but that's not the only buzz. There's the reaction you get from people who have felt stuck for years who suddenly see that all they needed to do was shift their thinking and, hey presto, the problem disappeared.

You solve one problem, you've solved them all

When you solve a problem at its root-cause, you not only remove one unwanted effect, you remove all the unwanted effects that stemmed from that one root-cause. It's like pulling a spreading, sucker-spawning weed up by its root. It stops all the surface growth in one strike. For any overworked manager who has too much to do and too little time to do it in, the opportunity to achieve such a major return on the investment of time it takes to uncover and remove the core-conflict can't be ignored.

Building impressive mental muscle

Everyone has problems, in all areas of their lives. The real difference between people who are happy with their lot and those who aren't isn't the absence of problems, it's the presence of a positive attitude and the self-confidence to know they can solve them. Self-confidence comes from experience of solving problems. If you've got problems, it's good to know that the grass is only greener on the other side because the person on the other side has developed tools and techniques for keeping the grass green! But it doesn't have to be us and them – anyone can build their problem-solving muscles. And using a tried and tested problem-solving technique that gives impressive results is the best confidence builder of all.

And great relationships too

One of the things I like most about getting stakeholders together to tackle the root-cause problem-solving process is that the process itself does much more than just make the problem disappear. There's no finer experience to be had at work than being part of a group of people doing the kind of breakthrough thinking that leaves everyone on a high – the relationships forged in those circumstances are the kind that you can rely on.

Making limited resources go further

Have you ever wondered how much time we waste trying to deal with problems at the level of their surface symptoms? In most root-cause problems I've dealt with there have been at least a dozen unwanted effects all of which were problems in their own right which people had been working on in isolation for a long time. I don't know about you but I'd rather solve one problem than twelve – and even if my approach takes twice as long that still leaves me better off. By tackling problems at their root-cause, you free up so much time for yourself, your staff and colleagues that it's hard to imagine why anyone would want to do all the busy work that's involved in skating over the surface. And that's without mentioning the prevention aspect – new problems that would have spun off from the root-cause won't now come up and therefore won't need a new, ingenious solution of their own.

No more shabby compromises

I think I've probably said enough about my dislike of shabby compromises not to need to go over it again here. I'll just say it's a real pleasure to see a group of stakeholders who got everything they needed without having to give something up to get it.

Changing from a 'can't-do' to a 'can-do' culture

And if all this isn't motivation enough, working with this problem-solving process actually changes what's in people's heads about problem solving. I've seen it switch on some of the biggest cynics I've ever known and I've seen people go from feeling completely disempowered to becoming real 'can-do' types. When you bring a problem-solving group together, you're not only solving the problem, you're giving people a learning experience that enhances their capability to solve problems and their belief in their power to solve problems.

Above all, it's a chance to get your logic and intuition in sync

There's something about most working environments that seems to keep us in 'either/or' mode. Half the time, we're afraid to say we have a gut instinct or a bad feeling about something because so many organizational cultures place the emphasis on hard facts and cold logic. And the rest of the time we're so overworked that we don't have time to slow down and make a considered judgement so we end up flying by the seat of our pants, leaping from one instinctive reaction to another hoping that when we have time to reflect we won't be sorry we listened to our gut. The reality is that neither of these options is ideal but if you can find a way of solving problems by bringing your logic *and* your intuition into play . . . you'll be a great problem solver and a great manager.

Towards a way of managing for the new era

The beliefs that help me make sense of my world and the people in it, including me

Beliefs come before action – and inaction!

Columbus had to believe the earth was round before he could set sail to prove it and the same applies to us in everything we do.

People do what makes sense – even when you can't tell from their results

How many times have you reacted to someone's actions with, 'But that doesn't make any sense'? We can believe human beings are irrational or we can believe they do what makes sense but that everyone's 'sense' is different. It's easier to make sense of what people are doing if we stop thinking our logic is *the* logic. Have you ever wondered why you did something that got the opposite effect to what you wanted, even though you knew all along what would happen?

If we were conscious of everything we know, our logic would be clearer to us

Sometimes, a new experience that has similarities to an earlier experience will trigger something from the vast store of experiences we keep in our subconscious. When we do this with people, it's prejudice – literally prejudging them based on previous experience that might or might not be relevant. Have you ever taken an instant dislike to someone then, when you got to know them, liked them? What triggered your initial response? Did they remind you of someone else you didn't like?

Our subconscious alerts us through our intuition

When our subconscious mind wants to tell us there's something we've forgotten, that's relevant to the situation we're currently in, it uses our intuition. Have you ever listened to someone saying something that sounded logical which you still felt absolutely sure was wrong yet couldn't explain how or why?

Except when it skips that step and drives us straight to a knee-jerk action

Taking an instant dislike to someone is an example of our subconscious bypassing the intuition alert stage and driving us straight to a response. When our responses don't seem logical to our conscious minds, we fear being irrational. But as I said, people always have a logic – it just isn't always a conscious logic!

We don't fail, we just achieve an intention we didn't know we had

Have you ever tried to give up a bad habit and failed? Did you blame lack of will-power? If your conscious and subconscious have conflicting intentions, your subconscious will win because it's stronger. What might you have to gain from not giving up your bad habit? Or what might you have to lose from giving it up?

Our needs drive our intentions and our beliefs drive our behaviour

Our beliefs tell us how to behave to meet our needs. Like everything else we've ever learned, we learn our beliefs from our experience. What are you not doing that you know you should, because you believe it will be a painful experience?

Our experience is created by our subconscious

There's a lot of rubbish talked about people creating their disability, which is a hurtful mistake people make who don't realize there's a difference between an event and an experience. Have you known two people who were at the same meeting (event), describe it so differently (experience) it was as if they'd been to different meetings?

Which always has its own logic – even when we can't see it

One of the main functions of our subconscious is to keep us feeling sane. The lengths it will go to is probably why it's often called the creative subconscious – as in creative accounting maybe! It governs everything from the things we notice in the first place – have you ever bought a new car only to suddenly start seeing that model everywhere you go? – to the way we interpret events to create our experience.

Our logic comes from our beliefs

My logic will only make sense to you if we both believe that the same (a) causes the same (b). If you believe that smoking causes lung cancer and I believe there's no connection, we'll never agree on why there's rising incidence of lung cancer among people in third world countries who are encouraged to smoke by unrestricted advertising practices because we'll be analyzing using different logics.

Our ingrained beliefs stem from childhood experiences of pain and pleasure

We form many of our beliefs in childhood, which is a pity because that's when we're worst equipped to interpret events. For one thing, we're dependant on parents to meet our needs, which means we learn to associate pleasure and pain with how they react to the way we behave to get our needs met. As adults we can say, 'Well that's one way of looking at it, dad, but it's not the only way' but as children, if a parent reacts like we've done a bad thing, we've done a bad thing, period, and that belief stays with us until something forces us to re-examine it, if it ever does. What's your most painful childhood experience? What has it taught you to believe?

We use those beliefs to interpret later experiences

As a teenager I got to stay up past my bedtime analyzing history with my mother. And whenever I was upset about anything she would tell me to pull myself together and try harder. I learned that brains were 'in', emotions were 'out' and that if at first you don't succeed, try harder and never quit. For many years, I was more Mr Spock than Captain Kirk and I genuinely believed my worst experiences were those when I acted on my feelings not my logic. What about those childhood beliefs you've just identified – do they still influence the way you interpret events? [Aside – for anyone concerned for my mental health, I've cracked the 'emotions are okay' thing and I'm working really hard on giving up my stubborn refusal to quit even when I'm flogging a dead horse. I'm not there yet but I'm not going to quit until I succeed. Oh dear, maybe I'm not doing as well with that one as I thought.]

And we learn to judge ourselves according to the feedback we get

My British History teacher used to give me A+ and read my essays out to the class praising my 'delightful prose' (oh, the shame). My European History teacher used to give me C– and suggest caustically, 'A few more facts and a little less verbiage wouldn't go amiss'. Do you have a behaviour that's admired by some and criticized by others? In judging it, whose views matter most? If you ignored what others think, how would you rate it?

But other people's judgements of us often tell us more about them than us

I bet you learned more in the last example about my history teachers than about me. What about the people who admire and criticize your behaviour? What do their judgements tell you about them?

So we need to learn to reframe

When I lived in Brixton, I saw a poster with two photographs on it – the first, a narrow angle shot of a black man running along a crowded street with a white policeman running after him and the second, a wide angle shot showing both the black man and the policeman chasing a third person. It was challenging people who assumed the black man in the first shot was a criminal, rather than a plain-clothes policeman, and showing them that they were seeing what their prejudice wanted them to see, not what was there.

When is a strength a weakness? The times it doesn't work for you

Are you sceptical about the things I'm saying? Is scepticism a strength or a weakness? When someone has to anticipate negative reactions to their proposals, scepticism can be helpful. When they're responding to radical ideas from team members by dismissing them without consideration, it's probably a weakness. How we judge a characteristic often depends on what our experience of it has been. Have you found scepticism generally helpful or hindering in your experience?

Competence is often a matter of being a round peg in a round hole

I'm not saying we don't have strengths and weaknesses. I'm saying they're just a reflection of how well we fit our operating context. My favourite ever boss was widely acknowledged as a visionary, brilliant strategist and future 'youngest ever' managing director. Yet, though he'd been a good enough middle manager to get promoted, there'd been nothing to indicate how exceptional he was to become. In a middle management 'implement other people's strategies' role, he was a round peg in a square hole but in a director's role, he was in his element. What were your best and worst jobs? How did your characteristics fit your best job and how were they a mismatch in your worst job?

To get our interpretations right, we have to slow down our judging process

Taking a more neutral approach doesn't mean no judging. We need to make judgements to move forward. What worries me is the speed with which we leap to judgement and the fact that once decided, we lay our judgements down in our subconscious, start to live by them and forget to take them out for review. And once we've made a judgement, our RAS ensures we only see things that reinforce the rightness of it (the sanity thing again). Given these consequences, it doesn't seem unreasonable to spend a bit more time wondering and exploring before we judge.

And take the time to listen to ourselves

Whatever we're doing, we're doing two things in parallel. Our conscious mind is doing the activity and our subconscious mind is watching us do the activity, making sure our actions are in line with our intentions and triggering alarm bells when they aren't. Listening to our alarm bells is the one sure way we have of staying on the right track.

It's not just characteristics that are neutral, it's events

A friend who'd been in the same job for twenty years was made redundant. He said at the time it was the worst experience of his life. Now he says it was the best thing that ever happened to him because it made him stop, take stock of his life and think about what he really wanted to do. And now he's doing it and is happier than ever. Did the event go from bad to good? No, his interpretation changed. It's natural to judge events quickly. It gives us closure (what a yuk word) which allows us to move on but which also stops us learning everything the event has to teach us. Have you ever had a bad experience that you later believed had been good for you?

And emotions

Speaking as a former Mr Spock, I'm fascinated when people describe emotions as bad (anger and hurt) or good (happiness and love). Emotions exist to tell us something about an event. Anger, for example, is triggered by someone breaking a rule that we live by or trampling on a value we hold dear. Assuming we've interpreted correctly, anger tells us to put something right that's gone wrong. It's not our emotions that get us into trouble, it's our autopilot responses. Have you ever used anger, in its righteous indignation form, to right a wrong?

And pre-programmes

I have a pre-programme about consultants that says they come into the organization, talk to staff, write up our ideas (the ones our managers wouldn't take seriously when we told them) present them back to our managers (which the same managers now take seriously because they heard them from an expensive suit) and walk off with a small fortune. My autopilot response to this pre-programme involved saying as little as possible to them. Recently, though, I've worked with a number of consultants who've not fit my subconscious expectation. Pre-programmes can be valid at the time we lay them down in our subconscious but times change and we forget to bring them out and check to see if they still hold up. Do you have a pre-programme about a group of people that you formed years ago? Are you sure it's a true reflection of your current experience of that group?

And even beliefs

Do you believe in the 'do as you would be done by' golden rule? Have you heard George Bernard Shaw's riposte 'Do not do unto others as you would they should do unto you. Their tastes may not be the same'? As someone who likes to know where I stand with people, it took me a while to realize there are people who'd rather not know – if where they're standing is a bad place. The golden rule can be helpful as a last resort with strangers (a kind of 'if in doubt, do as you would be done by') but there's no excuse for being in doubt with your staff – just ask them! Have you ever done as you would be done by and got short shrift?

The difference between the 'push' and 'pull' approach to managing change

When we're consciously trying to change something (I'm trying to give up interrupting people) we're in 'push' mode, trying hard, working from our conscious mind. When we give up trying to force change and set our intention on being different (being a better listener) and then just observe ourselves in action, we bring our subconscious mind on board and it gently 'pulls' us towards our new intention. Have you ever set your heart on something impossible, not really worked on it, but still found all sorts of help coming your way?

We need to listen to our fears

We live in a world governed by 'feel the fear and do it anyway' sound-bites. Well, let's forget the twenty-first-century pop psychology culture for a moment and think about why we have a fear mechanism. Fear is part of our survival instinct, designed to prepare us for fight or flight. It's there to tell us we need to act. If we don't listen consciously to our fears, our subconscious will listen and sabotage our efforts anyway, so we might as well.

And to the people who push our buttons

For years I've been irritated by status conscious people. It wasn't until I looked back and realized I'd left one job when the organization became open plan and I lost my office and another because some people on my level were re-graded to a higher level that I discovered a status conscious streak I'd denied for years. What irritates you in other people? When do you display the same characteristic? If you don't believe you have it, ask someone you trust if you have it before you dismiss what I'm saying.

And to our characteristics

Most people focus on their weaknesses and take their strengths for granted. A friend of mine counted listening as a strength, so he listened more than talked in meetings. His boss (who could win an Olympic medal for talking) branded him a poor performer because he didn't make much impact. If my friend had spent more time thinking about how his listening hindered his performance, he might have done something to improve his performance in meetings. What might you do differently if you really listened to your characteristics?

And to the standards we set ourselves

We all have an **internal regulator** that maintains our standards at the level our subconscious thinks is right for us, based on our beliefs about ourselves. Its job is to pull us up to our standard when we slip back, and to drag us back when we get above ourselves. If we don't think highly of ourselves, we settle for lower standards than we're capable of, or we push ourselves to achieve perfection – either way, we feel bad about ourselves. We can't change our internal regulator until we change our beliefs about ourselves.

What are your standards on tidiness at home? Do you feel you have to tidy up when visitors are due? Or do you always tidy the mess they make as soon as they've gone? If we don't think highly of ourselves we settle for lower standards than we're capable of, or we push ourselves to achieve perfection – either way we feel bad about ourselves.

And to the lessons in the experience we create

I had a colleague who believed all men were sexist. Whenever they used the masculine gender as a catch-all for both sexes, she'd tell them to say 'he stroke she'! They made fun of her and she ended up with a negative experience. I preferred to have fun at their expense. I was fond of saying things like 'I'm a man of my word' and watching their reaction – which was comical. By taking their position and exaggerating it until it became funny, I made them think about language without making them feel bad about themselves and, in doing so, created a different experience of them.

So we can find the beliefs that help and hinder us

Sometimes our beliefs are buried so deep in our subconscious, we don't even know we've got them. Looking at our experience can give tell us what we believe. Remember that bad habit you failed to give up? If I asked a neutral observer, 'What must my reader believe (about themselves, others, the world at large) to have created the experience of failing to give up that bad habit?' what would they say to me?

We all have an internal cast of characters

I have a friend who's a real monster at work but completely henpecked at home. Another who runs her own company but turns into a clinging child when her partner is going away on business. And a middle-aged friend with a 'rebellious teenager' streak who likes to drink twelve pints on a Friday night even though he can't take his drink like he used to. I have a 'repressed child' who pops out at and emotes at people when my feelings are being ignored. Who's in your cast of characters? What provokes one of them to make an appearance? Which ones do you like and which ones do you try to ignore?

And a dark side that can shed great light on our performance

Whatever you want to call it, we all have a person we're afraid we might be but hope we're not. We have two tactics for dealing with them – if we're conscious of them, we hide them by wearing masks.

> A **mask** is something we pretend we are to cover something we are pretending we aren't. I have an arrogant streak I don't much like so I wear the mask of openness about things I'm not good at. It has a positive effect on others (they become open too), so I think of my mask as the positive side of my arrogant streak.

If we're not conscious of them, we project them onto other people. What characteristics don't you like about yourself? What masks do you wear to cover them up? How do your masks help you? How do they hinder you? Who gets to you in ways they don't get to other people? Which characteristic of yours might you be projecting onto them?

We're **projecting** when we see in others some 'thing' [a thought, belief, characteristic or whatever] that we have in ourselves but don't see and wouldn't like if we did [which is why we don't]. Our subconscious wants us to be mentally healthy, which means accepting every part of us, so it keeps showing us the bits we deny by projecting them onto other people – the ones who push our buttons. That person usually has the 'thing' in a small way, enough of a hook to hang our projection on, but not enough to justify our reaction. One of the best ways of knowing if you're projecting, is when the person who pushes your buttons doesn't do it with others. That's when you know your reaction is telling you more about you than the person you're reacting to.

And coping strategies – though some work better than others

How do you cope with criticism? Do you get angry and defensive or listen politely and then ignore it or feel hurt or rush to explain yourself or criticize the person right back or sulk for a few days then do something about it? If you listen, take on board what's useful, ignore the rest and feel good towards the person doing the criticizing, I probably picked the wrong example for you. I'd like to meet you though as I've never met anyone who doesn't use a coping strategy for criticism. What kinds of situations do you not like dealing with? What coping strategies do you use? They protect you but do they have negative effects?

We influence others by acting out our subconscious expectations

My former colleague acted out her subconscious expectation of men being sexist through her attitude and behaviour and their subconscious responded to what she was giving out. Many organizations have so many rules, they create a subconscious expectation that managers should act like parents and treat their staff like children. As an adult, I don't expect anyone to check I've cleaned my teeth, so how come at work, we spend so much time checking the work of our staff? The more we act like parents, the more we are acting out our subconscious expectation that our staff will act like children, and the more we will create that subconscious expectation in them. No wonder we don't get excited by the prospect of empowerment programmes. If you empower children, it's all freedom and no responsibility. How do you treat the people you manage? Do you trust them to get on with the task or check up on them all the time?

And they let us – by transferring their power to us

In an organizational hierarchy, people tend to act on their subconscious expectations about authority and power. So, staff expect the manager to know the answers and, in doing so, give away their power and help sustain parent/child relationships.

We also influence by the way we reward and sanction the responses we get

I once knew a woman who could win medals for 'red penning' reports. Whenever one of her team writes a report that doesn't read well, instead of giving it back to them to rewrite or coaching them, she rewrites it herself. What do you think her team members are learning? What do you do when someone produces a poor-quality piece of work? And we don't just reward poor performance, we punish good performance. I know someone who gives all his rush jobs to the person he trusts most. Some reward! What happens in your organization to managers who do good work?

What we focus on expands – so we need to choose carefully

When I wanted my direct reports to improve the way they managed their teams, I started asking them questions about their people management at our reviews for learning. It was amazing how much more they had to report as the months went by. Have you noticed that the better you become at something the more of it you do? The same thing happens when we focus on our fears. They expand and our subconscious thinks our intention is to avoid the fear becoming a reality.

We can't solve problems with the same beliefs that created them

One of my team had to design a fifteen-day training programme which over 3000 managers would be attending. He said it couldn't be done as with those numbers it would take years. It turned out he was thinking about training people in groups of twelve. I suggested we think about the problem not as training but as event management and we ended up with a conference-style approach which allowed us to train 200 managers at a time in a large venue with lots of facilitators. When was the last time you were stuck? What part of your thinking had to change to allow you to move forward?

And we can't change behaviour until we've changed the beliefs that underpin it

Behaviour is so influenced by beliefs there's no point trying to change people's behaviour. All that happens when we do is we set up a clash between our conscious (which is managing the new behaviour) and our subconscious (which is trying to keep us sane by getting us to continue behaving in accordance with our beliefs). Think about a bad habit you've successfully given up. What beliefs had to change before you could give it up?

It's our unquestioned beliefs lead to autopilot behaviour

Our bad habits tell us a lot about the beliefs we need to question. Think back to that bad habit you're trying to get rid of. What were the underlying beliefs? How long have you held them (how far back does your bad habit go)? How many times during that time have you reviewed them to see if they still hold true?

Asking the right questions transforms behaviour by transforming beliefs

Thinking is simply the process of asking ourselves questions and answering them. The trick to good-quality thinking is asking the right questions. I did a course with some twenty year olds. We had one lecture with a different case study every week. The lecturer shouted out the questions and we'd shout back the answers. Everyone thought they could analyze a case study because they could answer the questions. But the lecturer asked different questions for each case study and the trick to analyzing the case studies was in knowing the right questions to ask – but no one was focusing on learning from his questioning skill. Have you ever argued with someone and been unable to change their mind only to find that when you stopped arguing and started asking them questions, they changed their own mind?

If we want to create positive experiences, we have to 'sweat the small stuff'

People don't judge us on the big things; they judge us on their experience of us. We are much less about our major triumphs and disasters and much more about the person we show ourselves to be in those small moments of choice that happen countless times a day. Sweating the small stuff means thinking of the effect you want to achieve and the consequences of your actions before you make choices so that you make your choices – you don't let your choices make you. What makes you decide whether you admire someone?

And get off autopilot onto manual

Just because our brains like being on autopilot, doesn't mean we should let them. People aren't machines. Press the key on the computer keyboard that says T and T is what you'll get, every time. Speak to the same person in the same way two days running and, if their mood or circumstances are different, you will get a different response on day two than you got on day one. Does this tie in with your experience?

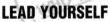

More power to your
[business-mind]

Even at the end there's more we can learn. More that *we* can learn from your experience of this book, and more ways to add to *your* learning experience.

For who to read, what to know and where to go in the world of business, visit us at **business-minds.com**.

Here you can find out more about the people and ideas that can make you and your business more innovative and productive. Each month our e-newsletter, *Business-minds Express*, delivers an infusion of thought leadership, guru interviews, new business practice and reviews of key business resources directly to you. Subscribe for free at

▶ **www.business-minds.com/goto/newsletters**

Here you can also connect with ways of putting these ideas to work. Spreading knowledge is a great way to improve performance and enhance business relationships. If you found this book useful, then so might your colleagues or customers. If you would like to explore corporate purchases or custom editions personalised with your brand or message, then just get in touch at

▶ **www.business-minds.com/corporatesales**

We're also keen to learn from your experience of our business books – so tell us what you think of this book and what's on *your* business mind with an online reader report at business-minds.com. Together with our authors, we'd like to hear more from you and explore new ways to help make these ideas work at

▶ **www.business-minds.com/goto/feedback**

[**www.business-minds.com**
www.financialminds.com]